ripoff
britain

ripoff
britain

and how to beat it

Edited by Phil Evans

WHICH?
BOOKS

CONSUMERS' ASSOCIATION

Which? Books are commissioned and researched by
Consumers' Association and published by
Which? Ltd, 2 Marylebone Road, London NW1 4DF
Email address: books@which.net

Distributed by The Penguin Group:
Penguin Books Ltd, 80 Strand, London WC2R 0RL

Contributors: Dave Attwood, Phil Evans, Chris Hayes, Andrew McIlwraith

The contributors and publishers would like to thank the following for their help in the
preparation of this book: Richard Balkwill, Diccon Bewes, Roy Brooker, Max Fuller,
Anne Harvey, Fraser Henderson, Paula Hodgson, Hilary Jones, Julie Lennard,
Johnathan Mitcham, Ajay Patel, Virginia Wallis, Kim Winter

This edition June 2002

Copyright © 2002 Which? Ltd

British Library Cataloguing in Publication Data
A catalogue record for this book is available from the British Library

ISBN 0 85202 898 9

For a full list of Which? books, please write to Which? Books, Castlemead, Gascoyne Way,
Hertford X, SG14 1LH
or access our website at www.which.net

Try *Which?* **magazine,** *Computing Which?*, **and** *Holiday Which?* **FREE.**
For more information on how you can enjoy a free trial of any of the above magazines
FREE – call 0800 252100
W2BV02

Editorial and production: Alethea Doran, Vicky Fisher, Robert Gray, Mary Sunderland
Cover design by Sarah Harmer

Typeset by Saxon Graphics Ltd, Derby
Printed and bound in England by Clays Ltd, St Ives plc

Contents

Introduction

This is not a book about rip-off Britain: it is about how to beat it. This guide does not set out to confirm all your worst fears and make you wish you lived somewhere else. It will, however, show you how to steer a steady course through many of the everyday markets you shop in and avoid retail robbery.

Counting the cost in the UK

Rip-off Britain has something for everyone, whatever the state of their finances. It is not simply a bible for those on a budget, but shows how to circumvent the problems that affect all of us who spend our hard-earned cash on goods and services in the UK. The book explains why we pay over the odds for so many goods, shows where to find loopholes in the system, and offers guidance on the best shopping methods and outlets.

By following our practical advice you can save time and money, enjoy stress-free shopping and gain an insight into how retail markets really work. The book will be invaluable if your means are limited – price reductions are a major concern if, for example, you have children to feed and clothe, or are elderly and have to heat your house for a large part of the day.

At Consumers' Association we believe the best form of consumer protection is having empowered, informed consumers driving a competitive market. When the general public ceases to be passive and starts to challenge retail forces and encourage competition, it benefits the poorest first and foremost – but ultimately everyone reaps the rewards. Impartial advice and access to the right information is crucial in order to get to grips with the complexities of retail markets. *Rip-off Britain* is based on independent research by *Which?* experts that will help you 'shop smart'. We can't pretend making savings is always easy, but with a little time and effort you will recoup at least the cost of this book and probably much more!

The story of the rip-off revolution

Almost every British consumer has a story about how he or she has been ripped off or short-changed. For many years, the fact that we paid over the odds for a host of goods and services – ranging from cars and CDs to credit cards and current accounts – was a topic of pub conversation and family get-togethers. What changed in the latter half of the 1990s was that people started translating this griping into genuine action. For a long time, many manufacturers and retailers capitalised on the fact that British consumers were happy to pay high prices because they valued 'service' and 'exclusivity', even though in reality these virtues were often in short supply. But with greater public awareness and an increased range of shopping options, consumers are starting to fight back.

So what changed? The overseas factor was one catalyst. Brits have holi-dayed abroad for many years and were often stunned by the low prices that they saw in other countries. However, travellers to some Mediterranean countries in the 1970s could make sense of the price differences by comparing the local standard of living and state of the economy. But the 1980s and 1990s saw two big new travel trends: channel-hoppers seeking bargains in the hypermarkets around Calais, and an annual exodus of sunseekers to Florida. Those of us who landed in the USA were struck by two things: firstly, that prices for many goods were considerably lower than in Britain, and secondly, the affluence of American society. Likewise, in Calais we saw a close European neighbour with a decent standard of living – and lower prices. What we learned on holiday we talked about in our pubs and at the school gate. We started to ask why Britain was so much dearer than the USA and France.

Shopping online – the preserve of a few until several years ago – was the second factor that helped to shift consumer opinion. Since the Internet embraced commercial concerns in 1994 it has revolutionised the way some of us shop. Today we can browse a mind-boggling array of sites without pressure from salespeople and order goods from abroad with minimum hassle. The number of 'mouse to house' addicts – from those who purchase the occasional travel ticket to people who buy all their books, CDs and groceries online – is growing fast, and it is predicted that by 2005 ten per cent of UK retail sales will be through the Internet. As well as being convenient to use and a great hunting ground for unusual items, many retailers' websites also lack the overheads of 'bricks and mortar' enterprises. This economic advantage, and vigorous price wars on the Web, mean that customers reap the benefit in savings. There are some real bargains to be had on the Internet – hence the large number of websites listed in this book. But bear in mind the caveats on pages 222–3, and don't assume online prices are invariably cheaper. It is always worth shopping around in 'real' stores as well.

As circumstances changed, the snowball started to roll; the citizens of 'Treasure Island', as Britain was so memorably dubbed, were getting angry. Frustration that so many areas of daily life were rigged and that little could apparently be done about it was publicly expressed for the first time. Sometimes this led to over-simplistic claims that entire markets were fixed – as was the case with media accusations against the supermarket sector. But in some cases it led to real action. A classic example is the new-car market. Here a combination of action by ordinary buyers, Consumers' Association and regulators in Britain and the EU has really made a difference. Prices have fallen and will fall further still. But most importantly, the desire of consumers to have a fair and properly functioning market seems finally to be feeding through to European regulators.

A positive outcome of this grass-roots rebellion is that some firms now consider competition a bonus, rather than a dirty word. In some fields, consumer anger about high prices is translated into action by companies that adapt to meet demand and undercut one another on price. Just look at the air travel market. For years there were claims that British Airways overcharged customers on many routes. In response we saw Virgin Atlantic stealing BA's thunder on US routes, and a boom in the number of no-frills airlines, such as Ryanair, flying to Europe. In clothing, Tesco and Asda have been the first to challenge restrictions on trade from outside Europe, while discounters such as TK Maxx and TJ Hughes have driven down the cost of buying high-quality branded goods. In cars, numerous online retailers and importers such as Broadspeed, Virgin Cars and Oneswoop have given consumers choice where before they had none.

Bad guys, good guys

Don't assume that all companies are out to fleece unsuspecting customers, and remember that in any market the same retailer may alternately play hero and villain. Retailers are as much the solution to rip-off Britain as they are the problem. For example, the supermarkets may sting us in some areas, but offer cures with CD, perfume and clothing bargains. For every bloc of overcharging car dealers, there is a car supermarket undercutting them.

Finally, big is not always best. In the CD market, for example, some of the best prices will come from the smallest stores and chains, and you often can't beat the expert advice you get from a specialist shop. Although this book concentrates on saving money, we recognise that sometimes you might want convenience over price, prefer service over speed, or feel like spending a little bit more to treat yourself.

Your retail risk

Each chapter in this book focuses on a specific retail sector. Your chances of getting ripped off vary according to how rigged or inherently risky each area is; in some, you need to really work hard to get around the problems that are placed in your way. Sectors that come with a hazard warning and require healthy levels of suspicion are cars, clothing, CDs and DVDs, telephones and mobiles, credit cards and current accounts. Moderate-risk markets are airfares, toys, perfumes, electrical goods, computers, mortgages, train tickets, gas and electricity bills and loans – here you simply need to exercise caution and think carefully before you make decisions. The final category, where the chance of getting fleeced is relatively low provided you follow sensible advice, comprises food, books, car hire and hotel rooms. Chapter 15 looks at loyalty cards, affinity schemes and flight schemes (which let you make money while spending it) while Chapter 19 outlines your basic legal rights when shopping.

How to use this book

This guide is designed to help you find your way safely through the maze of marketing hype, sales pitches and plain confusion that envelops many markets. We don't cover everything – just those sectors that present particular problems or where caution is needed. It is our intention to explore other areas in future editions.

Each chapter provides some basic information on how the market in question operates, including the legislative or economic forces at work. The key to getting around a problem in the marketplace is to understand why it is there and what you are dealing with: forewarned is forearmed. Next we explain how to negotiate the stumbling blocks and get the best deal. Useful telephone numbers and websites are given throughout the book, but note that the list is not meant to be exhaustive. We highlight (mostly nationwide) retailers that we know provide at least a partial solution to the problem, but this is not to say that other retailers will not do as good a job – your small, local specialist may well deliver the best results. The book also provides advice on what to do if something goes wrong with your purchases, and how to shop online safely.

All website addresses and telephone numbers are correct at the time of going to press.

Whenever you hit the shops or trawl the Internet in search of bargains, remember this general advice:

- **Don't believe the hype** Always be sceptical of advertising.
- **Safeguard your rights when buying from any company** (even those we recommend) by following the advice in Chapter 19.
- **Accept that you can't win 'em all** Some markets require wholesale reform before they can become consumer-friendly.
- **Buying cheaper does not mean poor quality** Inexpensive goods and services are not necessarily inferior to higher-priced items – the retailer may simply have a different supply line or more competitive pricing policy.
- **Bargain-hunting can be fun** Shopping is now considered a leisure activity, and nabbing a bargain can add to the enjoyment!
- **Push your luck** Try haggling with your retailer – you never know, it might just work.
- **Don't get in over your head** It's easy to focus on the savings you make when bargain shopping, but you have to be able to afford your purchase(s) in the first place. Keep tabs on what you spend and make sure you don't over-stretch your finances.

The debate surrounding rip-off Britain has helped to galvanise British consumers into taking action to overcome obstacles in the marketplace. The aim of this book is to make that task easier. If we all join forces against the markets that cause us problems, then we can stop them being an issue. Tell us how you get on; what worked and what didn't, and what markets you think we should cover next time. Our email address is books@which.net.

Phil Evans
Principal Policy Adviser
Consumers' Association
May 2002

CHAPTER 1

Airfares

The commercial airline market is complicated, but whether you are considering a short hop to Europe or taking a longhaul flight there are some good bargains to be had.

The economics of the industry mean that we see competitive, cost-cutting practices on a day-to-day basis, such as discount flight centres and no-frills carriers. However, the different types of option open to consumers who want to purchase a ticket – booking your flight as part of a package deal, through a travel agent or directly over the Internet – can be confusing. The number of stages that get between you and your airline seat also add to the complexity, as does the fact that, as with all services, you have to rely on someone else to provide most of the information to you. It pays to do a little digging and understand the system.

Cutting the cost

To get the best deal on flights, follow these general tips.

Book your flight separately

Booking your flight separately from other elements of your holiday or overseas stay can work out as a very cheap option, provided you play your cards right – it's also possible to save money if you book your hotel independently (see Chapter

13). More and more people are arranging their holidays this way rather than plumping for a package.

Beware of first-screen syndrome

Beware the curse of the first screen! When you ask a travel agent about a flight, the chances are that he or she will look on a Computerised Reservation System (CRS). These computer databases were originally developed by the airlines to help them manage their own flights. The flights that pop up on the screen first tend to be those of airlines that fly direct to a given destination, listed in alphabetical order. Next come the indirect flights. The connection to the CRS is a precious thing for travel agents and they tend not to like to look too far into it to get a flight option. This is both because the connections tend to be quite slow at peak times and because the agent generally knows it is unlikely that consumers will want much more than the first available flight on the screen. It is an accepted industry fact that over three-quarters of flights get booked from the first page, and around half of all flights from the first line of that page. It is unlikely that, without prompting, a travel agent will search the entire database for options.

Travel agents can access details of flights on no-frills airlines such as easyJet, but may charge you a booking fee of about £10. It is best to approach these companies direct (see pages 18–19).

Fly indirect

Direct flights by the main carriers – which tend to be the 'national' airlines of the countries between which you are travelling – for example, British Airways, Air France, Lufthansa, Alitalia and Iberia – are often the most expensive (although this may not be the case if you book through a consolidator such as Trailfinders (☎ 020-7938 3939).

If saving money is more important to you than the speed of your journey you could ask about indirect flights. These are flights that involve you taking a more roundabout route to your destination. Sometimes this can be a short wait for a connecting flight at an airport on the way (for example, connecting in Zurich on the way out to Mumbai), or a much more circumspect route which stops in a number of places to find connecting flights.

Insurance warning

If you fly indirect watch out for problems with insurance cover. Your policy may not cover your whole journey, especially if delays occur – and the more connections you have, the greater the risk.

Find out who flies on the route

It pays to find out all of the airlines that fly to where you want to get to so you can compare prices and make savings. For some destinations this is relatively straightforward. For others this can involve a good deal of digging. The best way to investigate the options is to put details of your trip into an online travel service such as Expedia (**www.expedia.co.uk**), Travelocity (**www.travelocity.co.uk**) or ebookers (**www.ebookers.com**). These services tend to come up with most of the airlines and most of the routes available to you. The bulk of the website information comes from scheduled carriers. However, a number of sites, such as Travelocity, do allow charter flights to be checked – but remember that these can have inflexible timings based around the package travel holiday times. Another way to find out about flights is to look in the *OAG Flight Guide*, available in libraries. If you are meeting a travel agent face to face and he or she offers you the first flight on the screen, be sure to ask about the other options.

Investigate the old colonial links

The route networks that the airlines operate have developed because of historical and political factors, and reflect the pattern of emigration and immigration between countries. Thus you will find well-developed links to the Indian sub-continent in the UK and great links to Francophone Africa from France. Knowing about such connections can be particularly useful if you are not flying out of the UK or are prepared to be flexible about your departure point.

You don't need to be a history buff to benefit; simply buy a guidebook for where you are going to. You will almost always find a potted history of the country – this will give you a reliable indication of which countries are likely to offer good air services to that destination.

Think alliances

Increasingly, some of the major airlines have started up 'alliances' which share anything from routes to booking systems and even aircraft. There are two big alliances: OneWorld (**www.oneworld.com**), which includes British Airways, American Airlines, Cathay Pacific, Finnair, Iberia, Lan Chile, Aer Lingus and Qantas; and Star Alliance (**www.star-alliance.com**), which comprises 14 airlines including British Midland (BMI), Air New Zealand, Air Canada, SAS, Singapore Airlines, United and Lufthansa.

Alliances can be both a good and a bad thing; in theory they can lead to higher fares and less competition on routes in which the airlines used to compete. But where airline alliances connect airlines together, they can lead to both lower fares and easier and better connections. You may find that the place you are heading to is served by one airline in an alliance. If you want to break your journey or take a trip to a destination 'beyond' your final one you may find that the alliance will give you a good deal as a result. This also applies to round the world trips.

Be flexible

It can pay dividends to be flexible and willing to travel a day (or sometimes even just a few hours) before or after your ideal time. Insisting on travelling out of a busy business city early on a Friday evening or first thing in the morning will guarantee high fares, for example. It is well worth checking out flight costs on alternative days – the easyJet website (**www.easyjet.com**) shows you prices for the days before and after the one you have requested.

Be prepared to travel in the middle of the week or at weekends and keep an open mind about who you fly with. One of the good things about airline alliances is that you can mix and match airlines and destinations. So, for example, instead of flying direct to a city a long way off you can go via another with relatively little disruption and possibly a significant fare saving.

Consider breaking the journey

If you are going on a long-haul flight it is worth contemplating breaking the journey. As soon as you do this, you open up the possibility of choosing from a wider range of airlines and services, and seeing a city you may not have thought of visiting. This can lower your costs and get you on to a better airline. For example, if you decide that you want to fly to Australia and choose not to go directly (directly in this case means stopping for a couple of hours to refuel and stretch your legs), you are faced with options such as Emirates via Dubai and Singapore Airlines via Singapore. Both these airlines come out very near the top of the Which? Airline survey carried out by *Holiday Which?* (the latest of which was published in March 2001) and offer very cheap stop-overs in their home cities to entice travellers. The length of stop-overs is usually flexible – if you are in a hurry you can be whisked from one plane to the next, while the advantage of stretching this to a day or two is that you can experience a new city and country.

Cutting the cost on transatlantic flights

If you are flying on a transatlantic route to the USA it might be worth comparing prices on the airlines that fly direct

---

Airfares where less is more

You would not expect a return flight and hotel stay to cost less than the return airfare to that destination. However, some airlines strike this sort of deal – known as 'inclusive tour' (IT) packages – with flight specialists in a bid to fill planes. The best bargains tend to be on flights to destinations such as Thailand, Malaysia and Singapore although you will also see (less dramatic) savings if you visit New York, Australia or Cape Town. Late bookers travelling off-season may find the biggest savings.

It is always worth enquiring about inclusive tour fares. Ask an agent for the cheapest direct return flight and get from London airports (BA, Virgin, United and American Airlines from Heathrow, and Continental and Delta from Gatwick) and elsewhere in the UK. Birmingham, Glasgow and Manchester all offer a small number of direct flights to the USA, with Manchester ahead of the pack.

As well as the regional option, you should also think about the airlines that pick up passengers in London airports on their way from somewhere else. For example, at the time of writing you can fly to New York from Heathrow on Air India or Kuwaiti Airways (en route from India or Kuwait), and Air New Zealand does a London–Los Angeles route on flights that eventually end up in New Zealand. Because these airlines are largely dependent on passengers from the original port of call travelling half-way around the world, they are often able to offer very low fares to fill the seats emptied at the stopping-off point in London. If you want to save money this way, it might be worth going direct to agents that specialise in Indian or New Zealand flights for tickets to

---

them to add in a few nights' accommodation. *Holiday Which?* found that this approach could shave £100 or more off a flight to Bangkok in winter 2001.

The companies below are a good starting point: alternatively, scan the weekend travel supplements for more numbers.

Bridge the World	☎ (0870) 444 7799
eBookers	☎ 020-7757 2324
Thomas Cook Direct	☎ (0870) 750 0132
Trailfinders	☎ 020-7938 3939
Travelmood	☎ (0870) 500 1002

the USA, as they may have better access to the booking systems of these airlines. Check the weekend and evening newspapers and look for adverts that claim a specialisation in a specific country or region.

If you're not flying from London, you could try flying into continental Europe from your nearest airport to travel to the USA. Flights into Amsterdam's Schiphol airport (via KLM UK, easyJet, BA and others), Paris Charles de Gaulle and Frankfurt (via British Midland) are pretty frequent and provide access to good route networks (see 'Think alliances', pages 14–15). In terms of the time taken, a connecting flight through Schiphol from Edinburgh will take much about the same time as one through London. Apart from convenience the main advantage of indirect flights is cost – the overwhelming majority of people flying to the USA from the UK go direct and the continental carriers will offer very attractive fares to tempt you on to their network.

Cutting the cost on European flights

If you're flying within Europe, avoid some of the traps of using a travel agent by booking directly with a no-frills airline (see below). Booking direct with scheduled airlines is rarely a good idea because of the higher cost (unless they happen to have a decent deal at the time you surf the Internet).

No-frills airlines

No-frills or low-cost airlines have become increasingly popular with UK consumers, and a large number of flights sold on these airlines are bought directly on the Internet. No-frills airlines to try are easyJet (**www.easyjet.com**), Go (**www.go-fly.com**), Buzz (**www.buzzaway.com**), Virgin Express (**www.virgin-express.com**), Ryanair (**www.ryanair.com**) and British Midland's bmibaby (**www.flybmi.com**). Booking direct with a no-frills airline has its drawbacks so bear in mind the following tips.

Don't assume low cost means low price

It may come as a shock for some punters when they log on to a no-frills airline site and are offered a return flight for a few hundred pounds instead of the £50 they were expecting.

All no-frills, low-cost airlines operate exactly the same system for selling seats as high-cost airlines (the 'cost' refers to the cost of running the service, not the ticket). They will sell the cheapest tickets first, and then assume that people booking very near the date of departure are getting desperate and are willing to pay higher prices.

Try to book well in advance to any destination as cheap tickets tend to go quite quickly. Leave it to the last minute and you might get lumbered with a ticket that is as expensive as a high-cost airline. Occasionally you can get cheap tickets just prior to departure, but this is not a safe route to getting on a flight.

Just because you are on the website of a low-cost airline, don't suspend your instinct to shop around. Very often you can find a cheap ticket on one of the scheduled airlines that is a reasonable competitor to the low-cost carriers – it may take a bit of time to ferret out the information but it is worth comparing. It is useful having one of the established Internet travel sites up (see 'Find out who flies on the route', pages 13–14) at the same time as the low-cost airline, so you can compare the deals on offer instantaneously.

Check the airport

To keep their costs low, some budget airlines (mostly Ryanair) fly to and from what are called secondary airports.

These tend to be smaller airports, often ex-military, which are further away from the town that they claim to serve than those you would normally expect to fly into. They might be a good number of miles from your destination – in other words, you might need to sit on a coach for an hour or two before you get to where you thought you were in the first place. This is not necessarily a problem, as long as you are aware that the airport may not be particularly convenient for the city you are travelling to. You shouldn't be misled about exactly where you're flying to – advertising regulators have cracked down on airline adverts, and operators now have to state the destination airport (if you don't know the name, check whether it is the main or secondary airport).

Beware hidden taxes

The price you are quoted should include all the taxes, airport and security charges that will be levied on your final ticket price. For campaigning reasons, a number of no-frills airlines (most notably Ryanair) make a point of adding these in right at the end of the process, to show how unfair they believe they are, which can lead to confusion on the part of the consumer. However, in advertisements all airlines and operators must quote the full price of a ticket, including taxes.

Make sure the website is secure

If you are planning to give someone your credit-card details, make sure the site is secure. For advice on safe shopping online, see pages 222–4. If you feel uncomfortable or unsure about what you are doing, phone the airline – most also take bookings over the phone (though you may have to pay more than you would over the Internet).

Make sure you read the small print

The same rules apply to online operators as to travel agents. Stay vigilant, always check the details of what you are buying, check your tickets and read the small print very carefully.

No package, no protection

If you're not buying a package, you're not protected by the Package Travel Regulations 1992, which offer protection in case the operator goes bust. Some flights are protected by an Air Travel Organiser's Licence (ATOL) – see page 229 for details of this and other DTI-approved schemes – but if you buy a flight directly from an airline you may have no redress if the airline goes bust. If you are worried, pay by credit card (you may be able to claim against the card company if the firm goes out of business), ask about failure insurance (often called 'passenger protection' or 'scheduled airline failure' insurance), or consider whether or not to book with the firm in question.

Further reading

Holiday Which? magazine covers the important issues affecting travellers. *Which? Holiday Destination* supplies key facts on over 60 countries and tour operator listings.

For a full list of Which? Books titles, see the back of the book.

CHAPTER 2

Books

The book market in the UK used to be underpinned by the Net Book Agreement (NBA), a voluntary price-fixing agreement dating from 1900, which meant that publishers fixed the price of the books in the shops.

In the face of growing discounting, and a formal challenge from the Office of Fair Trading, the NBA fell apart in September 1995. A number of publishers withdrew from the scheme and it was eventually declared illegal by the Restrictive Practices Court in March 1997. This meant that mainstream booksellers were able to offer discounts or special offers on particular titles. Nowadays there is much more competition in the market and promotional offers are available from various outlets, including supermarkets.

Cutting the cost

The place to look for a good deal depends on what sort of book you want. Books are sold in a wide range of different types of outlets: supermarkets, chain booksellers (such as Waterstone's and Borders), other high-street stores (such as WH Smith), small independent bookstores, second-hand bookshops, market stalls and even libraries. There are also book clubs, and, of course, online retailers. Each of these outlets is covered briefly below.

It is worth remembering that most books, particularly fiction and illustrated books, are published first in hardback, then later in (cheaper) paperback. How soon the paperback appears depends on how quickly the hardback sells – for bestsellers, the paperback may appear within a matter of months, so could be worth waiting for.

Bestsellers

If you want to buy a current bestseller you really can save money by exercising choice in where you buy it. Every large bookseller will tend to discount on the big names in fiction and non-fiction titles. They know that a new book from JK Rowling, Jamie Oliver or Stephen King will sell lots of copies. Some bookshops only discount their own big sellers, while some will use more accepted industry listings, although the former approach is more common. This can result in inconsistent offers on 'top 40' titles, so it pays to hunt around for the specific title you are after. Current best-sellers generally get discounted by a few pounds; this is true in supermarkets, book chains and general retailers. However, the biggest discounts on top sellers can be found online, at book retailers such as Amazon and BOL. Outlets such as these sell books at up to 50 per cent discount (see 'Online retailers', pages 27–9).

Classics

Copyright on UK-authored texts runs for 70 years after the death of the author. Copyright refers to the 'ownership' of the book's content, and is a form of intellectual property – a bit like a patent. It means that no-one else is allowed to reproduce the work without the copyright owner's authori-sation. Once a book goes out of copyright, any publisher can produce their own version. Therefore if the book you want was written around the turn of the twentieth century or before, there is a good chance that a number of different versions of the text will be available. For many of the classical texts, by authors such as Plato, Aristotle or Machiavelli, or English classics by authors such as Jane Austen, Dickens or Shakespeare, cheap editions are sometimes sold new for as little as £1.

It should be noted that the 70-year rule only applies to books authored in the UK. Other countries have different rules, and non-UK-authored books may come out of copyright earlier, making cheaper editions available sooner.

Academic and non-fiction books

As a general rule, the more obscure a new academic or non-fiction title is, the less likely you are to get a discount. However, there are exceptions. Most notable of these are those books that have large print runs and then fail to sell. These titles often end up in 'remainder' shops (see 'Discount bookstores', overleaf) fairly soon after publication.

Again, the online retailers offer some form of discount on academic and non-fiction books, although it may not be much.

Where to shop

The most obvious places to buy books are the big high-street book chains and the online retailers. However, there are also various less high-profile outlets where you could well find a good bargain.

Bookshop chains

Bookshop chains, general chains and supermarkets tend to adopt the same pricing strategy. The big difference is the stock policy. The larger book chains usually have more stock on the shelves and so a wider choice of titles.

Discount bookstores

Some bookstores deal specifically in 'remainders'. Remainders are the books that remain unsold after the initial sales push following publication – and they are the stock-in-trade of some chains and a number of smaller booksellers. Those books with huge, over-optimistic print runs, which then fail to sell, will be sold off in bulk to the discount trade. Other books to be found in these stores are imported from (mainly) the USA. These are titles that are not in production in the UK, or whose copyright has expired. The main bulk of the discount market is made up of art books and poor sellers in the general non-fiction market. Political biographies are another subject area often to be found here.

Most large towns will have some form of discount outlet. These are often small individual companies; no single chain covers a significant portion of the country. A number of larger stores in the main chains also have their own remainder sections, as do many independent booksellers. There are also several online book retailers which specialise in remaindered books (see opposite).

Independent bookstores

Although smaller bookshops have less shelf space than the larger chains and therefore are not able to stock such a wide range of titles, they are usually more specialised, so if you have a particular interest in a non-mainstream subject you may find that the staff knowledge and service in a bookshop that reflects this interest is of value to you. Remember that you can order any book, as long as it is in print, from any bookshop.

Second-hand options

If you are looking for a particular book that is fairly well-known (for example, a not-so-recent bestseller or a classic), and you are not fussy about buying a new copy, then it should be fairly easy to find second-hand. In addition to second-hand bookshops, markets and charity shops, it is also worth trying libraries, which all sell off old stock, either occasionally or continually. You can pick up second-hand books for as little as 50p, and usually for less than £6.

Book clubs

Book clubs offer reductions on a range of books and often publish their own editions of popular or classic titles, or specialist titles for hobbyists, at considerable discounted prices. They can be a good means of getting a bargain, if the books on offer appeal to you. The joining offer is generally very attractive, but you then have to enter into a contract with the book club. For example, you may have to buy a book a month for six months, or will at least be obliged to pay for those that are sent to you unsolicited unless you return them within a certain period of time. It is important, therefore, to read the small print.

Online retailers

Book retailers were the first to get a solid foothold in the online market. While an enormous number of bookshops have a web presence and a number of general retailers, such as WH Smith (**www.whsmith.com**), sell books on the Web, the online book market has come to be dominated by the 'big two': Amazon (**www.amazon.co.uk**) and BOL (**www.bol.com**). The advantage of online retailers is twofold: pricing is highly competitive, and discounts can be found on almost all stock. And, because it is not encumbered by high-street space restrictions, the range of stock available is vast. The most esoteric taste can be satisfied, often at a decent discount. Remember, however, that postage and packing is generally not included in the price, so it is important to always check the postage costs to make sure that they do not cancel out the savings.

In addition to the 'big two', another online retailer worth looking up is Alphabetstreet (**www.alphabetstreet.co.uk**). The site is very bright and cheerful and has a decent stock, although it is a little irritating in that prices are listed without reference to a recommended price; this can make it difficult to judge just how much of a bargain you are getting. Delivery charges are low.

All of the high-street chains have a web presence, although notably Waterstone's operates through Amazon! Hammicks has a rather unusual website (**www.hammicks.com**), which acts more as a shopfront for its specialist book stores (**www. businessbooks.uk.com**; **www.computerbooks.uk.com** and **www.hammickslegal.co.uk**). There is also a link to the more general Book Place website (**www.thebookplace. com**), which is a gentle, information-rich, introduction to the online book market. For academic texts, Blackwell's academic site (**www.bookshop.blackwell.co.uk**) is worth checking out, alongside Amazon.

The online remainder market is also a bargain-rich hunting ground. A large part of this market is the same as for the high-street discount stores (see above). One of the quirkiest online routes to discount books can be found at Bibliophile Books (**www.booksbymail.co.uk**). The online site mirrors the free newspaper that the company distributes every couple of months; prices are keen and stock is bought with some care. Other discount sites worth investigating are Book Bargains (**www.book-bargains.co.uk**), Postscript books (**www.psbooks.co.uk**) and Saxons (**www.saxons.co.uk**).

Further reading

For more detail, see *The Which? Guide to Shopping on the Internet.*

CHAPTER 3

Cars

The reason why we spend so much on new cars is clear. The manufacturers are allowed to restrict the means by which we buy cars: they can decide who can sell you a car and where they can sell it, and stop any other dealers of the same brand competing properly. This has the effect of artificially restricting competition *within* a brand, which has the knock-on effect of restricting competition *between* brands as no one has an incentive to compete for your money. This occurs at all levels – in your local area, where only a specified number of dealers exist for each brand; at the regional level, where you may have to travel significant distances to compare brands; and at the European level.

All of this creates a market which is effectively rigged by car makers to their own benefit. Where consumers are best able to undermine it, by shopping in other EU countries (such as Germany, Belgium and France), the manufacturers try to stop them, although they can get fined by the European Commission if they are discovered.

Britain has the disadvantages of a traditional lack of language skills and of being an island. In the recent past, consumers have tended to get a raw deal from such dealers on the Continent, who were very often in fear of the car makers who frown on sales to the UK from Europe. Because of this they would often find almost any excuse not to supply us with cars.

When the big appreciation of the pound against the euro (at the time of writing) is taken into account, a car price ratchet in the UK emerges – first by domestic firms jacking up their prices after being frightened by foreign imports, then by importers taking advantage of the action by the domestic firms. This situation got so bad that UK consumers woke up and started noticing the price differences abroad, which in turn led to a significant increase in personal imports and in shoppers using other intermediary operators.

Cutting the cost

Getting around the problem of high prices for new cars offers a number of challenges. The restrictive nature of the market means that beating the system requires both imagination and a willingness to go out on a limb for a bargain. However, if you are prepared to employ ingenuity and flexibility, solutions are available. These are divided into domestic and overseas options, although there is a good deal of blurring between the two. Your approach will also differ depending on whether you know exactly what model you want or don't mind. These options all require the consumer to do a bit of homework, but it's well worth being prepared when making such an expensive purchase.

The domestic route

When choosing a car in the UK, follow these basic tips.

Be open-minded

Never limit yourself to a specific group or sub-group of cars before you have explored all the options. For example, if you are after a car that can carry up to seven passengers you could look at the estate market as well as 4x4s or people carriers. This is because many estate cars are fitted with rear-facing seats at the back of the car to allow (small) people to sit in the car. Similarly, if you are after a compact town car you should not necessarily limit yourself to Smart cars and minis, but also think about some of the smaller run-about city cars like the Skoda Fabia.

Be open-minded about brands

You may favour one brand over another. However, you should not use that favouritism as a restriction, but as an anchor. A useful exercise is to place your preferred brand in the middle of a circle, adding competing models around it. This is not a method of rejecting your initial brand choice, but placing it within context. It also allows you to see the price difference between 'your' brand choice and its rivals. This forces you to ask yourself: 'How much extra am I willing to pay for this brand *vs* brand X?'

In order to establish which is the best (and cheapest) car for you, you should identify close substitutes to your preferred brand. This involves three stages:

- check out the car's 'family'
- check out its rivals
- identify the pecking order.

First, look at a suitable car family. These are groups of vehicles that share the same 'platform'. Platforms are the core of the car upon which the body and fittings are stuck. The platform method of production involves using a core number of components and parts to build different types of car. The range of cars built on the same platform can be relatively small (such as the VW/Seat/Skoda variations on the Golf) or vast (e.g. the use by Ford of the Mondeo and Fiesta platforms to churn out everything from Pumas to Probes and beyond). So if you are looking for a people carrier and you are struck by the Ford Galaxy, for example, you should compare the cars built on that platform: the VW Sharan and the Seat Alhambra. Similarly, if you like the look of the Citroen Synergie check out the Peugeot 806 and Fiat Ulysse. And if you are thinking of buying a VW Golf, check out the Seat Leon.

The next thing to do is check out the rivals to your preferred model by looking in the car magazines and seeing which cars are listed alongside your favourite. For example, in the executive car section you will see Mercedes listed alongside Peugeot 607 and the Nissan QX. Again, it helps to be broad-minded.

One of the faults of car makers is that they tend to engage in 'me-too' production. This involves entering into every product segment that there is, irrespective of their abilities in that area. For example, when Renault first entered the large people carrier market with the Espace, the car was pretty unique. However, within a few years the range of people carrier options was huge. Similarly, even in sectors dominated by one or two marques, almost everyone produces cars. Probably the best example here is the 'executive' car market – everyone produces, but only a few sell significant numbers. The 'me-too' factor is important when it comes to second-hand values and the sort of discount you might be able to get on a new price. For example, a new Vauxhall Omega is priced at a very similar level to the BMWs it competes with. However, as soon as it becomes second-hand it loses a massive amount of its value in comparison.

The third step is to place your brand in the overall pecking order of similar cars, such as 4x4s and people carriers. Any such ranking is bound to be subjective, but checking the car magazines will give you a sense of what is on offer. This can be difficult if you are partial to your choice being the top of the pile. However, note that sometimes the top brand in each sector gets away with charging a higher price than its rivals (this is called 'price leadership'). Indeed a car that costs more than its rivals usually provides a pretty good benchmark for ranking the rest. The pecking order should also give you an idea of which car is the pacesetter in the group and which manufacturers have to offer lower prices or higher specifications to sell their cars.

Don't pay over the odds for special editions

Be wary of paying over the odds for special editions, which may be described as 'exclusive'; in reality, this may mean little more than different seat covers and a fancy paint job.

Can you buy an ex-fleet car?

If you are trying to make savings, consider a nearly new ex-fleet car. The fleet sector is huge in the UK – much bigger than anywhere else in the world. The industry claims that just over half of the entire car sales are to corporate and car hire fleets, while *Which?* estimates that the 'real' retail sector (i.e. punters paying with their own money) accounts for only about 20 per cent of sales – thus, fully 80 per cent of UK car sales are financed by someone other than the consumer. This has major implications for the price that you, as a private consumer, end up paying. If you buy an ex-fleet car, it also has a significant impact on the 'residual' value when you either trade it in or sell it on (see pages 44–45).

Certain types of car, such as mid- and upper-level executive cars and family saloons, see very high fleet sales, while a broader range of vehicles is involved in the car hire business, which tends to favour the small city car, the mid-level saloon and the mass-market marques (e.g. Ford Fiestas and Mondeos). The mass-market producers – Ford, Vauxhall and to a lesser extent Peugeot, Renault and Nissan – sell a large number of cars to the fleet market.

Ex-fleet cars are commonly sold in car supermarkets (see pages 40–43), at auction and by second-hand car dealers. The downside to these vehicles is that drivers are likely to have loaded on the miles up and down the motorway. The upside is that the fleet owner is likely to have looked after them well.

Can you buy a pre-registered car?

Pre-registered cars are brand-new vehicles registered as 'sold' by manufacturers and dealers (now mostly the latter) to massage sales figures. These are the cars you see on the showroom floor with new number plates. It has been estimated that the number of cars pre-registered on a monthly basis can reach around 20 per cent of all cars sold. Some brands (such as BMW and Mercedes) pre-register relatively few cars, while others (usually Ford, Vauxhall and Nissan) pre-register a lot.

Some cars have a few miles on the clock, while some are used as pool cars by local car dealers for their staff to drive around in. These can end up with a couple of thousand miles on the clock and be legitimately sold as 'second hand'.

The big advantage with pre-registered cars is that they are cheaper to buy because they have already undergone depreciation – so you are buying the car at much nearer its true market value. For mass-market cars, the prices can be anywhere between 25 and 30 per cent cheaper.

Nearly new

There is no standard definition of 'nearly new', but it tends to mean cars up to six months old (in registration terms – not including time spent sitting on airfields!), and can include pre-registered cars driven twice around the block as well as ex-fleet or car-hire vehicles driven a considerably greater distance. Many cost much less than they would new, and may still be covered by a manufacturer's warranty.

Pre-registered cars can be found in a variety of locations. Franchise dealers are good places to uncover them – although they tend to be hidden at the back of the lot rather than put out front. Car supermarkets are also good hunting grounds for pre-registered makes. For more on where to buy, see pages 40–44.

The overseas route

Prices for most new cars are significantly lower on mainland Europe than they are at home. There are two ways of buying from Europe: going abroad in person or using an inter-mediary. The cheapest route in cash terms is the personal one; the cheapest in time spent is the intermediary. Cars bought outside Europe used to be mostly esoteric and avant-garde models, but increasing numbers have found a niche in the UK market – notably the Japanese versions of the Mazda MX5 (the Eunos), the Mitsubishi Shogun (Pajero) and the Toyota Previa (Lumina and Emina). For more details on Japanese imports, see page 43.

Do-it-yourself importing

A few years ago, importing a car from Europe was only for the adventurous and determined consumer. In the last few years, however, an increasing number of British consumers have taken the plunge and the process is less of a lottery than it used to be. Things you have to remember when importing personally include: ensuring that you get a car with the right British specification; you may need to ring around a number of dealers in the EU country concerned before you find one that will deal with you; and there are some paperwork and tax issues involved.

If you want to find which country in Europe is the best-priced for the car you want, you should start with the European Commission twice-yearly survey of prices. This can be found on **www.europa.eu.int/comm/competition/car_sector/** and a free hard copy can be ordered from the UK office of the EC on ☎ 0116-240 6803. The website is probably best because it also has links to manufacturers' phone enquiry points which are obliged to provide you with the contact details of their dealers across Europe.

You also need to bear in mind a number of other issues.

- You will need to build in a longer delivery time for your car.
- Deposits for Brits buying in Europe are often a lot higher (e.g. 10 to 30 per cent) than for buying at home.
- You have to take into account currency fluctuation – the time between paying your deposit and paying off the balance can be quite lengthy and the pound may have moved significantly against the euro by then. If the pound strengthens this is good news; if it weakens, bad; but either way it is a risk. Talk to your bank about setting up a foreign currency account to cover the balance, or contact

specialist currency hedgers (they advertise in magazines that specialise in car importing).

- Insurance for getting the car home can be a pain – contact your own insurance provider and see if it will cover you for bringing the car to the UK. If not, talk to the car dealer and see what they recommend. Alternatively you can pay someone to ship the car over to your door. This can cost a few hundred pounds but saves the headache of arranging insurance.
- You will have to complete lots of paperwork – which includes filling in special forms and paying the VAT on this. Contact the DVLA (☎ (0870) 240 0010, **www.open.gov.uk/dvla**) for details.

Using an intermediary

If you want to avoid the hassle (or fun depending on your view) of importing, you can get an agent to do it for you. You can deal with the established Internet retailers or use a specialist import broker – prices for both routes will be similar.

Many of the established importers (such as broadspeed, **www.broadspeed.com**) have been online for a while. New entrants into the online market include Oneswoop (**www.oneswoop.com**), Virgin cars (**www.virgincars. com**) and Direct Line's Jamjar operation (**www. jamjar.com**). Broker services usually allow you to tailor the service you want – from simply telling you which dealers on the Continent will sell to you, to doing all the paperwork and shipping for you. Check car magazines for adverts for brokers.

Whichever option you go for, make sure you are clear about the service you are paying for and speak to a few to get a sense of fees. With Internet importers, as with all online firms, make sure that you deal with companies which have clearly identifiable contact details. Go for those which ask you to pay a desposit directly to the Continental dealer or into an escrow account (a secure account that they cannot touch without your authorisation).

Where to buy

There are four options if you are shopping for a bargain in the UK.

The franchise sector

The franchise sector is a good place to find nearly new or pre-registered cars, though you may have to hunt around. Some franchise dealers will also import cars for you – although usually not of the make they are supposed to be selling! The willingness of dealers to admit that they have pre-registered cars varies from site to site and make to make. Some manufac-turers are displeased if their official dealers broadcast the fact that they have essentially brand-new cars at discount prices, while others will allow their dealers openly to advertise pre-registered cars. Persistence is worthwhile, even if it adds to the search costs for a car. It does not hurt to ask dealers of your preferred brand about pre-registered cars, as this shows that you know some of the tricks of the trade. You may be able to negotiate a discount with dealers.

Car supermarkets

Car supermarkets are a welcome addition to the car retailing market, and have helped to widen choice for the consumer. There are a relatively small number of car supermarkets in the UK. They tend to be very large sites housing a vast range of stock and are generally located near motorway junctions and outside major cities and towns. At these sites don't expect the cup of tea and chat of the franchise sector. The car supermarkets tend to operate on a 'pile it high, sell it cheap' motto, selling on cars at a low margin and aiming for volume. While this offers good bargains it does mean that you have to know what you are after before you go.

Car supermarkets

Autolink has branches in Maidstone (Kent) ☎ (01622) 661111, Chingford (Greater London) ☎ (020-8524 6060) and Southampton (Hampshire) ☎ (023-8077 8811), **www.autolink.co.uk**

CarLand Glasgow, Cannock (Staffordshire), Manchester, Lakeside (Essex), Enfield (North London), Chertsey (Surrey), Shirley (Hampshire), Sarisbury (Hampshire) ☎ (0800) 072 7059, **www.carland.co.uk**

The Great Trade Centre White City (London) ☎ 020-8969 5511, **www.gtccar.co.uk**

Motor Nation Garrets Green (Birmingham), Widnes (Cheshire) ☎ 0121-786 1111, **www.motornation.co.uk**

Motorpoint specialises in new cars and has branches in Derby ☎ (0870) 1254321 and Burnley ☎ (0870) 1240000, **www.motorpoint.co.uk**

Trade Sales Direct Slough (Berkshire) ☎ (0870) 127 3763, **www.trade-sales.co.uk**

Car supermarket sites have started to sell pre-registered cars, but focus mainly on ex-fleet vehicles, so you will find a good smattering of mid-market Fords and Vauxhalls. You will also find a limited number of people carriers and some smaller models. It's worth noting that you can also pick up a decent executive car with the 'wrong' badge – such as a Vauxhall Omega or Nissan QX. It's a simple fact of the car market that some badges will demand a premium (such as BMW and Mercedes), while others (such as Vauxhall and Nissan) do not have the same prestige. If you are not an out-and-out badge snob, this means you can take advantage of others' snobbery!

Supermarkets are ideal for knowledgeable consumers and those who have a clear idea about what they want. They are also ideal for comparison shopping as some of the larger sites group vehicles by type (i.e. people carriers, saloons and city cars) rather than brand. This allows you to compare within your chosen category.

The process of buying at a car supermarket is different to buying at a dealer. The customer is left to browse without being put under pressure to buy – many car supermarkets state that their salespeople are encouraged to be as unobtrusive as possible. Don't go to a car supermarket determined to haggle on price. Most operate a system which is closer to that of standard supermarkets than car dealerships.

It's also worth looking at adverts in motoring magazines to get an idea of sales outlets and current deals.

Dealers *vs* supermarkets

It's worth comparing the prices and extras on offer at dealers and car supermarkets. Car supermarkets are generally cheaper as their out-of-town premises can help to keep prices down (*Which? Car 2001* found that the smaller, more customer-friendly supermarkets tend to be more expensive than the larger ones). However, dealers sometimes offer the best deals on an ad-hoc basis and may be open to negotiating discounts.

Both supermarkets and dealers offer a range of services to encourage you to buy. These might include free servicing and insurance, free tanks of petrol and even free mobile phones. Trade-in price guidance and finance packages (usually from third parties) are often available too. Some outlets offer independent car inspections from breakdown organisations such as the AA (☎ (0870) 600 0371, **www.theaa.co.uk**) and RAC (☎ (0870) 533 3660, **www.rac.co.uk**) but you can also organise these yourself. Warranties are usually offered but, as with any warranty, it's important to check carefully what they cover and for how long.

Niche operators

The vast majority of the second-hand car market is made up of niche operators – for example, dealers that sell only very cheap cars (i.e. those under £1,000), 4x4s, people carriers or upmarket cars. These kinds of operators can be found in most local areas – check pull-out sections and advertisements in the local paper.

This sector includes import specialists. Some focus on the EU market, either bringing in new cars or acting as intermediaries to source imported cars. There is a smaller market in the import of Japanese cars to the UK. The mainstay of this business has been esoteric or 'cheap' alternatives to established brands, and vehicles designed to compete with the more expensive UK versions of established Japanese models. The reason such imports have succeeded is that the Japanese versions are very often considerably better specified than the European version. This has added to the price advantage of second-hand Japanese cars and in turn kept down prices of the UK models. There are some technical difficulties with importing a Japanese vehicle, but a decent importer will sort those problems out for you.

Any car coming into the country from Japan will need to complete a souped-up version of the MOT called the SVA. All Japanese cars will require modifications such as having the speedometer changed from kilometres to miles per hour, and most will need changes to their lights and to the neck of the fuel tank. For more detail on Japanese imports and a list of dealers, contact the British Independent Motor Traders Association (BIMTA) (☎ (01892) 515425, **www.bimta.com**).

Shopping online

Buying a car over the Internet tends to be only for the brave and those clued up about technology. However, it is a choice that an increasing number of people are taking. As described above, the Internet has helped to broaden access to cheap and imported cars. Broadspeed (**www.broadspeed.com**), Oneswoop (**www.oneswoop.com**), plus Virgin cars (**www.virgincars.com**) and Jamjar (**www.jamjar.com**) all offer slightly different services: some offer just imports, while others will offer whatever bargains are available at the time that you log on. In addition, Autobytel (☎ (0800) 7831514, **www.autobytel.co.uk**) generally acts as a shop window for franchise dealers, but also offers good second-hand deals and exclusive online prices. A good research site for checking out second-hand car deals is the online version of Autotrader (**www.autotrader. co.uk**).

How to avoid depreciation

One of the biggest costs of owning and running a car is the depreciation in its value over time. This is particularly true of new cars. Just driving a new car out of the showroom can reduce its value by 12 per cent. And in the first two years, a car can lose nearly 45 per cent of its value. As a car ages, the rate of depreciation slows down, but over the first six years your car might lose around 75 per cent of its value.

If you are buying a new car, the type of car will affect the level of depreciation (see box below). The best way to minimise the effect of depreciation is to buy a second-hand car instead of a new one, so you don't bear the costs of the spectacular fall in value in the early years. Subsequent loss of value is very similar across makes.

Depreciation tips

- If you are buying a new car and plan to sell it on or trade it in after a few years, then look for one that has low depreciation. However, if you plan to keep the car for many years then depreciation may not be a major consideration.

- If depreciation is an issue for you, steer clear of the most basic and most expensive models offered by the manufacturer, and go for a mid-range vehicle.

- Typical company fleet cars are prone to rapid depreciation, whereas some small cars, especially those with power steering, and luxury makes such as Audi, BMW and Mercedes-Benz, tend to hold their resale value better.

- Buy a used car in good condition, or consider a nearly-new car such as an ex-demonstration model with low mileage.

- Make sure that your car is regularly serviced, and keep a full service record, to maximise the resale value.

Cutting costs on car parts

You can frequently make savings of around 30 to 50 per cent on the price of spare parts by buying from independent dealers rather than from franchised dealers. You don't have to buy the manufacturer's spare parts, unless this is a particular condition of your warranty. Many of the independent spare parts on the market are similar – or in some cases identical – to the manufacturer's parts, and as long as the part you buy is made by a reputable manufacturer, there may be very little difference in quality. All independently made parts should carry a guarantee. Beware of buying parts from less-established sources such as car boot sales however – some very cheap parts may be counterfeits.

Buying from a dealer

A franchised dealer should stock or be able to order the part you require. It's unlikely that prices will vary much between dealers in different areas.

Independent dealers include parts shops, repair garages and high-street chains such as Halfords (☎ (0800) 197 1196, **www.halfords.com**). They usually sell a range of common spare parts for popular makes of car. If you need a more obscure part, it's possible that they may not stock it, in which case you may have to buy it through a franchised dealer. Prices of independent dealers can vary greatly so it is worth shopping around.

Buying from other sources

Be wary about buying spare parts from boot sales or markets. Some trading standards officers have raised concerns about the safety of inferior-quality counterfeit parts being imported into this country.

Reconditioned parts

Some dealers – both franchised and independent – may quote an exchange price for certain parts, such as starter motors, alternators and clutches. If you give them your old worn-out part, they will replace it with a reconditioned part at a reduced cost. Reconditioned parts should be as reliable as new ones and come with a standard guarantee. If you specifically want a new part, you may have to ask for one, but you probably won't get an exchange price for it.

Quality control

The selling of car spare parts is a lucrative industry and a number of large companies make a wide range of parts for different makes of car. Some make dedicated branded parts for car manufacturers to sell through their franchised dealers, but may also supply identical (or very similar) parts to the independent parts replacement market, to be sold under another name, and often for a much cheaper price.

All genuine spare parts will carry a guarantee from the part manufacturer. Legally, the garage fitting the part is responsible for ensuring that it is of satisfactory quality and fit for its purpose.

If you have a problem with a part you have had fitted, your claim may be against the garage rather than the parts manufacturer, depending on the nature of the problem. If the part has a manufacturer's guarantee, you could also claim against the part manufacturer.

Don't be short-changed by your garage

If you're concerned about any parts a garage is fitting, ask to see the packaging and documentation that it came with to check that it does come with a guarantee. You could also ask to see or keep the old part that has been replaced to check that it has actually been replaced and that it really needed changing.

Warranties

If your new car is covered by a manufacturer's warranty (usually one to three years after purchase), check its terms and conditions carefully. Many people think that, to keep a warranty valid, you have to have the manufacturer's parts fitted by a franchised dealer. However, in most cases, fitting independent parts should not invalidate the original warranty – but any independent parts you fit will not be covered by this warranty.

If you have an extended warranty, dealer warranty or mechanical breakdown insurance (MBI) on an older car, the terms and conditions may be different from the manufacturer's warranty. Most extended warranties are in fact MBI policies. Although you may buy the policy through a car dealer, your contract is with the insurance company. The policy may contain a condition that insists you have the car serviced and repaired by a franchised dealer. Failing to abide by the terms of the contract may mean you're not covered.

If you're having parts fitted at the same time as having your car serviced, you should check any warranty or insurance documents carefully.

Forthcoming changes

The great news in the car market is the European Commission's announcement in early February 2002 that it was going to liberalise the market and inject more competition. The bad news is that this change will not really start to happen until towards the end of 2003. With luck we will see some relaxation in advance of the new rules coming into play during 2003. The advice in this chapter will apply until that time.

The changes to the European car market should be far-reaching although caution needs to be exercised, as the car industry is adept at getting round rules that are supposed to force it to deal fairly with consumers. The EC is proposing that dealers will be able to sell more than one car brand, much more easily than they can now. If prices are out of kilter across Europe then dealers from one country will be able to set up in another and sell cars at the prices in their home country. Thus a Belgian Ford dealer could set up in Dover and sell cars at Belgian prices. Rules on where dealers can set up and how they compete will also be loosened. All in all the EC have done British consumers a great favour. Only time will tell if it has cracked this rip-off market.

Further reading
Which? Car is a complete guide to buying a new or used car, published every year by Which? Ltd.

CHAPTER 4

Car hire

From the claims made in advertisements by car hire companies, it seems that hiring a car has never been cheaper. To hire a car for under £10 a day is enough to make you wonder whether it's worthwhile owning a car as opposed to simply renting one when necessary. However, the pricing of car hire is far from transparent, and companies frequently levy an array of extra charges that bump up prices far above what you might expect from the daily charge quoted. This chapter explains how to keep prices low whether you are hiring a car in the UK or abroad.

Cutting the cost

If you can find the right deal, hiring a car in the UK can be a quicker and cheaper alternative to using public transport. Some large hire companies offer a 'One Day/One Way' option which can be an attractive alternative to a cramped, delayed train journey for a family travelling a fair distance.

In order to get the best deal, follow these general tips.

Don't assume big is bad

Prices vary a great deal between different companies operating in the same area. For example, smaller independent operators are generally cheaper than the multinationals – look in the *Yellow Pages* for details of those in your area.

However, special promotions often mean that it's worth-while checking out the rates offered by Avis, Hertz and their competitors, even if there are other, smaller, companies nearby.

The big boys

Avis ☎ (0870) 606 0100, **www.avis.co.uk**

Budget ☎ (0800) 181181, **www.budget.co.uk**

easyCar ☎ (0906) 333 3333 (calls charged at 60p per minute), **www.easyCar.com**

Europcar ☎ (0870) 607 5000, **www.europcar.co.uk**

Hertz ☎ (0870) 844 8844, **www.hertz.co.uk**

You could also try getting a quote from the companies whose websites are listed on page 57 (under 'Go online if you can').

Check out franchise dealers

Try to get prices from at least four companies, including two major players, one independent and a franchise car dealer. Many franchise dealers will hire out brand new vehicles that are not selling too well and make a few quid from the hire fees. In some areas, franchise dealers that hire out cars may be easier to find than car hire outlets. The easiest way of getting a quote is to look on the Internet – all the major companies have sites that can give you an instant quote.

Be consistent in your demands

When obtaining quotes, make sure that you're comparing like with like: specify the size of car you want, ask if the quotes include VAT, and check the level of insurance cover offered. With smaller companies, ask how many miles are included in the basic rates, and what the extra rate is if you exceed that mileage.

Check for extra charges

Bear in mind the following possible extra charges when looking into the cost of car hire:

Additional drivers

Some companies will levy a charge if there is to be more than one driver of the car. Make sure you check who is going to do the driving, particularly on a long trip, and make sure they are covered in the price.

Out-of-hours collection

You need to think about the time that you will pick up and drop off the car. If you are doing either out of normal office hours there might be a penalty.

Fuel costs

Car hire companies generally require you to return the car with a full tank of petrol. If this is not the case, the charge that they levy to fill the tank is far higher than you would pay at the pumps yourself so it makes sense to get your own petrol. Make sure you know which deal you are getting into and don't get stung for exorbitant refuelling charges.

Include all the extras

If you need vital extras such as child seats, roof racks or ski racks, mention these when enquiring and do your best to book them in advance since it's generally cheaper and will avoid any problems with availability.

Check the car

Make sure that you look the car over carefully – using the
company's checklist and diagram – when you pick it up. Car
hire firms will often bill you for even very small amounts of
damage to the car. In March 1993 *Which?* found instances
of companies using the checklist system unfairly by
expecting hirers to inspect vehicles to an unreasonable level
of detail – which unfortunately can still hold true today.
EasyRentacar, in particular, was a subject of concern after
several reports of customers being charged for damage that
they felt they were not responsible for. After consultation
with the Office of Fair Trading, the company now asks
customers to witness car inspections or sign a form
confirming their refusal to be a witness.

Bear in mind that checklists and signed acceptance forms
do not absolve hire companies of their responsibility to
supply safe vehicles in good condition. Companies should
not require hirers to spot anything more than is likely to be
visible on a quick viewing of the vehicle.

However, to minimise risk, before signing the contract
carry out these straightforward checks. Not only might they
help you avoid having to pay an unnecessary cost but they
will also improve your safety.

Tyres

Ask for another car if you find bald patches in the tread, or
cuts and bulges in the side walls. If any of the tyres appears
to be flat, ask for the pressure to be checked. Ask the
company to show you where the spare tyre and jack are
kept. Demand a replacement if the spare is bald, cut or
bulging.

Bodywork

Point out any dents, scratches or damage to the interior, and have faults recorded on the contract to ensure that you are not charged for existing problems when returning the car.

Washers and wipers

Check that any windscreen washers and wipers work.

Seat-belts

Check that all belts fit comfortably and click securely into the catches. Tug sharply on inertia belts to check they lock. If there will be more than two passengers or someone has to travel in the back, make sure rear seat-belts are fitted.

Controls

Ask the hire company to demonstrate any controls on the car that you are unfamiliar with — such as wipers, alarms, hazard warning lights — and ask for a copy of the handbook for that model.

Lights

Ask someone to stand outside the car to confirm that the side lights, dipped and main beams, indicators, brake and reversing lights all work properly.

Brakes

Try out the brakes by having a test run around the car park or block before setting off any further. Check that the brakes don't pull to one side.

Contact number

Make sure that the company provides a contact telephone number in case of any mechanical problems with the car, or in the event of an accident or other emergency.

Cutting the cost abroad

The popularity of fly-drive deals and the plethora of ads in travel supplements is testimony to the fact that pre-booking a hire car is big business. Booking from the UK can reduce the amount you pay, but if you're thinking of hiring a car for a holiday abroad you need to bear some general advice in mind.

Book in advance

Be wary of leaving the arrangements until you've arrived at your destination. Car hire can often be more cheaply arranged via a UK-based company such as Holiday Autos (☎ (0870) 400 0099, **www.holidayautos.co.uk**), though clearly this depends on the exchange rates at the time. Additionally, booking in advance ensures that all your requirements – child seats, etc. – will be available on your arrival.

Beware 'free' offers

Be cautious about 'free car' or 'rental-free' offers that are optional parts of a holiday package. These deals can exclude handling fees, surcharges, taxes and other extras, and work out more expensive than a similar deal you could find yourself.

Take note of price promises

Look out for price promises when shopping around to get the best deal. Many UK-based companies promise to beat all competitors' rates and it's well worth playing one off against the others to get the price down.

Go online if you can

The Internet can be a useful tool when you are looking for a good deal on car hire in another country. Sites such as **www.travelocity.co.uk**, **www.ebookers.com** and **www.autoreservation.com** can provide you with instant quotes after you've answered a few basic questions about your requirements. You can also try nominating the price that you're prepared to pay for car hire at **www.priceline.co.uk**, where the company will trawl its network of well-known car hire companies to see if it can find a deal that fits your price limit. Holiday Autos has a particularly well-designed website with a straightforward booking process at **www.holidayautos.co.uk**. It features 'week-enders' and 'late deals' sections and also gives you a discount of £10 for booking online.

Try out the airline tie-ins

Budget airlines such as Go (**www.go-fly.com**), Ryanair (**www.ryanair.com**), Buzz (**www.buzzaway.com**) and easyJet (**www.easyjet.com**) all have arrangements with car hire companies to provide discounted deals for their passengers, so it's well worth getting a quote from their websites if you are flying with these airlines.

Make sure you have enough insurance

Car hire deals in the UK generally include all the insurance you're likely to need. However, hiring a car abroad involves giving consideration to other forms of insurance. You should be familiar with the types on offer and be careful what you sign up to – commission-driven staff at car hire companies traditionally have a hard-sell approach, and it's easy to become confused, particularly after a long flight. If booking from the UK, make sure that you enquire exactly what insurances you're agreeing to as part of the package.

The insurance you will *definitely* need is collision damage waiver (CDW) insurance. This is the insurance provided by the hire company to cover damage to the car. It often carries an excess (the first £100 of repairs, for example) and may exclude certain parts of the car, such as the tyres. CDW is sometimes called loss damage waiver (LDW) in the USA.

States where you won't need LDW

If travelling in the USA you should always take out LDW unless you are hiring in Illinois or New York State, where state laws make the hire company liable for the vehicle apart from the first $200 in Illinois and $100 in New York State.

The insurances you *might* need are:

- **Theft protection** Accept this if it's offered – otherwise you leave yourself open to punitive costs if the car is stolen.
- **Supplementary liability insurance** Also known as 'top-up' insurance, this covers you if you injure someone or damage property or other vehicles. In Europe, the standard contract with the hire company generally provides sufficient 'third party' liability cover. In the USA however, it's essential as the liability cover that comes as standard with a car hire contract is very limited. Don't rely on your travel insurance – virtually all policies specifically exclude liability involving 'use or possession of any mechanically-propelled vehicle'. Take out supplementary liability cover to give $1 million of protection. You can do

this most conveniently through the hire company, but you can also arrange this cover more cheaply with a broker before you travel.

The insurance you *won't* need is:

- **The hire company's personal accident insurance** This duplicates the cover you may have under a life insurance scheme. And your travel insurance should give you cover for injury or death. It should also cover medical expenses and baggage and belongings.

Pre-book for better redress

One of the advantages of pre-booking car hire with a company that has offices in the UK is that it's easier to complain if something goes wrong and you can't resolve the problem on the spot. Language difficulties are avoided, and the company should have a complaints policy as well as a Code of Practice enforced by the British Vehicle Renting and Leasing Association (☎ (01494) 434747). Remember that if you book a car as part of a fly-drive deal, or as part of a package holiday, you will have a contract with the British tour operator. Under the Package Travel Regulations, such tour operators are legally responsible for their suppliers, so you can take up any complaints directly with the tour operator if necessary.

CHAPTER 5

CDs and DVDs

CDs

For many years UK consumers have paid more for CDs than consumers in the rest of Europe and much more than those in the USA, Australia and Hong Kong. Yet compact discs are technically the same wherever you buy them. It does not matter if you buy one in the USA or Hong Kong, it will work in your CD player in the UK.

There is no one reason why we pay so much. One of the main reasons, until quite recently, has been the fact that no one in the marketplace had the incentive to discount. The UK CD market was supplied by a small number of record labels which sold via a small number of specialist and more general retailers. Neither the labels nor the retailers saw any reason to offer better prices to consumers and so the prices went up. However, things began to change. The supermarkets started taking a closer interest in the CD market and began selling the top 40 CDs at a discount with some success. Then Internet retailers got in on the act. While some (notably Boxman) failed, a number of the more established online stores have prospered (see overleaf). Consumers began to notice that CD prices were far higher here than in the USA, say. At the same time the smaller niche labels, which saw little reason to join the high-price club, were penetrating the dance and classical music market.

Cutting the cost

The Internet, for once, is actually fulfilling its promise – some of the best stores are actually online incarnations of established offline retailers.

Buying online

The advantages of the Internet are many and varied in the world of buying CDs. The key benefit is a lower cost of doing business (shipping from a shed in the middle of nowhere as opposed to high rent in the high street leads to lower prices for the consumer). The shed doesn't need to be on the high street or in a shopping complex close to consumers and it can carry a much wider and larger stock than a retail store.

The price and availability advantages of the Internet retailers are thus twofold: heavy discounting on top-selling artists – usually centred on top-40 sales lists (here high volume offsets lower margins) – and lack of shelf space constraints, which means that non top-40 artists enjoy better access to the market at reasonable prices.

Prices between niche specialists and the generalists tend to be similar for most stock, although generalists are often able to discount the top 40 more effectively, while specialists may offer special deals on back catalogue.

The two major online book and CD sellers, Amazon (**www.amazon.co.uk**) and BOL (**www.bol.com**), offer a good range of CDs. They also tend to include cover graphics for all CDs and often provide 30-second snippets from selected tracks on the CDs. This is useful for consumers unsure whether the album on view is definitely the one that they want or had on vinyl (for those old enough to remember it!).

This places Amazon and BOL at an advantage (in display terms) over specialists. such as 101cd (**www.101cd.com**) which displays only minimal information on each CD.

Another site worth checking out is Play 24/7 (**www. play.com**). The site has a rather erratic stocking policy for CDs but is good value (the prices quoted include delivery). Although the company is based on Jersey in the Channel Islands, stock is shipped from the USA so remember to double-check the track listings (differences sometimes occur between US and European CDs).

Two retailers in particular seem to have got the business model working well in their selected niches. CD Wow (**www.cdwow.com**) operates almost solely as a top-40 retailer and prices are very low (often £8.99 per CD) with postage and packing free. This is because it sources and ships from Hong Kong where CDs are both very cheap and not subject to import restrictions (which makes sourcing from Indonesia, for example, easy). The range is not broad, although some speculation on a pre-release basis means that some titles are discounted even lower than £8.99. You need to check whether the CD you want has all the tracks you would expect. The site usually indicates if it is a different specification.

The other site which offers a good choice is Tower Records' (**www.towerrecords.co.uk**) online venture. It does not matter if you log on to the US or UK site as the search option provides all prices and sources available. The advantage of using the UK site is that it lists all UK-sourced CDs for each artist first and then proceeds to list the US CDs quoted in pounds. CDs from any source (the site includes Japanese imports where available) can be placed in the basket and ordered as if they were from the country you are sitting in. This allows you to buy a US version of a CD for a significant saving over the UK version. Waiting time can be a little longer for US imports, and you run the risk of having to pay duty on the imports, but the savings can make it worthwhile. The second major advantage of the Tower site is its breadth of stock. The listing of UK and US availability allows you to access CDs that may not be available in the UK. Other online ventures of established chains (such as **www.hmv.com**) could learn from this combination. Virgin Megastores does not yet operate an Internet service in the UK; the US sites used to ship but appear to no longer do so.

DVDs

The digital versatile disc or DVD has been hailed as the future of home entertainment. The discs, similar to CDs, store huge amounts of information and can deliver much better picture and sound quality than VHS videos. The fact that the film is on a disc means that the producers can be more flexible in the way that they deliver the material. For example, many DVDs offer a menu at the first point of loading that allows you to choose to watch the film, or to listen to the soundtrack or watch a documentary. The best DVD releases will contain a number of special programme extras ('featurettes' and interviews) that make viewing as much an education as an entertainment.

The DVD was to be the first truly universal film mode. Like the CD the DVD would do away with the complexities of the video market and allow any film to be screened on any machine anywhere. However, this did not take into consideration the profits of the film companies which release films at different times in different parts of the world and like to maximise their revenue in each individual market. The last thing they want is for a blockbuster release in the UK to be undermined by the DVD being released in the USA at the same time. The world was divided up into different regions and DVDs coded to play only in that region. The division was designed to protect the film companies from a global trade in DVDs that would force prices down to the lowest level. It also planned to allow them to stagger the release of movies in line with the regional formats.

Regional codes for DVDs	
Region	Restricted to
0	No restriction
1	USA, Canada
2	Europe, Middle East, South Africa and Japan
3	South and East Asia (including Hong Kong)
4	Latin America, Australasia and the Caribbean
5	India, Pakistan, Africa (excluding Egypt), Russian Federation, North Korea and Mongolia
6	China
7	Not used
8	Special venues such as planes and cruise ships

What this meant in reality was that DVDs sold in the USA would simply not be playable in the UK and vice versa. Consumers were thus left with a restricted choice of where to buy their films. This led to price discrimination between markets, a problem that affects UK consumers particularly badly. This meant, for example, that the same DVD that might cost the equivalent of £10 in the USA would cost £15 in the UK; and there was nothing that the UK consumer could do to get around this.

The actual encoding process is a simple one – the DVD has a tiny bit of information on it that tells the DVD player the region for which that DVD has been sold. The DVD player reads that code and compares it to its own – if it matches you can watch the film – if it does not – you can't. The content of the DVDs may vary. Some US Region 1 DVDs have many more extras than the European releases.

Cutting the cost

The good news is that there are a number of ways around the problem of higher DVD prices. With some background knowledge the canny consumer can negotiate a path through the price maze.

The hardware

The most important step in circumventing high DVD prices comes with the choice of machine on which to play the discs. The route to take here depends on whether you have a DVD player already. If this is the case, two possible approaches are open to you – hacking and chipping. Hacking the machine involves accessing sometimes hidden menus on the software built into the machine. Chipping the machine involves cracking open the machine and physically changing or adding a component. Bear in mind there may be drawbacks (see below).

Hacking
To hack the machine you will need to access the software that drives the player and instruct it to become a multi-region machine. Some machines allow you to do this at the setup stage on the handset and some afterwards, although the latter are far less common. Some manufacturers, however, make their machines almost impossible to hack.

These include big names such as Sony, Sanyo, Toshiba, Panasonic and Pioneer as well as Denon, Goodmans, Teac and Technics.

The problem is that you are unlikely to know in advance how to hack your machine. The answer can come from three sources: the retailer, the Internet and magazines. If the retailer is a specialist then it is likely to know *if* you can hack the machine software and more importantly *how* to do it. Some even provide the information up front. Always ask the retailer how to make the machine multi-region – if the retailer doesn't know go somewhere else! Another important source is the Internet. Here you will find a number of sites and suppliers that will provide advice on how to make your machine multi-region. Some magazines will also provide information in their reviews section on how to make the machine multi-region.

Chipping

Chipping the existing machine, while more physically demanding, is probably more straightforward. This is because most people will go to a specialist to do the job, rather than try it themselves. Chipping involves inserting a chip into the machine that turns it from a region-specific to a multi-region machine. If you are a technophile you can contact suppliers of these chips directly and fit it yourself; if not, contact an independent firm that can do it for you. Listings for a good number of these firms can be found in the back of most DVD magazines on sale. Some retailers or service departments will do it for you, but their charges can be very high. Also remember to check the wording of the warranty or guarantee.

If you don't own a machine

Life is pretty simple! Buy a multi-region machine. These fall into two categories:

- machines that are capable of simple modification
- machines that are automatically multi-region.

The first category is a generic machine that can be set up by the retailer or purchaser to act as either a restricted or unrestricted player. The machine is the same wherever it is sold (save for plugs!) – so the most cost-effective means of production is to have identical hardware and software that only requires a minor modification at the point of sale. A good retailer will leave this modification and offer the consumer the choice to make the machine multi-region. Some retailers advertise the machines as capable of being made multi-regional and often even advertise how.

The second type is the simplest to deal with as it is automatically multi-region. Such machines often come from manufacturers that you may not have heard of, or from a manufacturer that is not tied to the bigger film studios. These machines will often require no work on the part of the consumer. The best will simply scan the DVD that has been inserted and play it, bypassing any regional coding. The multi-region machines often cost slightly more than region-specific machines but can work out cheaper than the high-street 'normal' machines.

Where to buy a machine

The high street is not a recommended place to find multi-region DVDs or machines that come with multi-region hacking advice. The high-street chains tend to sell region-specific machines only and seem unaware of the multi-region issue. It is therefore advisable to seek out specialists.

To find independent electronics retailers which specialise in multi-region DVDs, check out the advertisements in specialist DVD magazines. They will often also review machines and even provide advice on how to hack a machine.

Richer Sounds (☎ (0870) 900 1000, **www.richersounds.com**) tends to specialise in last season's stock or overstocks. The staff always tell you what the status of the product is (i.e. cancelled order, last season's stock etc.). Discounts can be significant, and the regional coding issue is clearly addressed. This chain also stocks other audio electronics and hi-fi separates.

The DVDs

As mentioned above, the regional coding for the DVD drives was designed to allow film companies to stagger their releases. Most films are on general release in the USA ahead of their release in the UK. This situation has changed a little, thanks to the fact that multi-region players have become so popular. This can often mean that films are released in the cinema in the UK just ahead, or even at the same time, as films get released on DVD in the USA. As with all products with an initial publicity hit, a large volume of the sales of DVDs will occur just after release. As sales decrease over time, prices are often reduced to entice new customers. Because the sales cycles are out of kilter between the USA and the UK this means that current releases in the UK may have been on sale in the USA for some time – and thus the prices of the DVD in the USA may be a lot lower.

However, this is irrelevant unless you can get hold of the DVD from the USA (presuming you have a multi-region player). Fortunately, this is a lot easier than you may think.

Ex-rental DVDs

You can get excellent deals by buying ex-rental DVDs. Blockbuster, for example, sell very new releases for £9.99. The website **www.channelfilms.co.uk** offers ex-rental DVDs at bargain prices. You may get a box with 'Rental Copy' printed on the spine, but the quality of the disc should be as good as new. Blockbuster guarantee their disks for one year.

Buying online

Because of the popularity of multi-region DVD (and therefore the unpopularity of regional coding) several sites now sell regionally coded DVDs. Some sites, such as CodeFree DVD (**www.codefreedvd.com**) have links to retailers, while others will sell region 1 (US) DVDs to UK consumers directly. Among the best are Play 24/7 (**www.play.com**) and Tower Records (**www. towerrecords.co.uk**). The latter, as with CDs, lists all returns for a DVD and states whether it is Region 1 or 2 and will ship both. Play.com quotes prices inclusive of postage, which is handy if you want to avoid duties. Movietyme is a US-based company which has a UK-targeted website (**www.movietyme.com**). Movies are all Region 1 titles and quoted prices include postage. Check the small print about delivery times and conditions of carriage. You should bear in mind that if you order DVDs from overseas there may be handling and import charges to pay.

As recommended above for the players themselves, the best place to find information about Region 1 DVDs is from magazines. Most DVD magazines now have listings and reviews for both Region 2 (European) and Region 1 (US) DVDs. For some reason, differences exist in the actual content of the DVDs, and the magazines will often also compare and contrast DVD releases to indicate which one offers the best value. The magazines with the biggest Region 1 reviews sections are also the ones with the most adverts from suppliers of DVDs —so have a browse before buying. Most websites linked to DVD magazines are largely just enticements to subscribe. The DVD Review (**www.dvdreview.net**) site is an exception and provides reviews of machines and releases and some good links and a calendar of upcoming releases.

Because of the popularity of importing DVDs from the USA into Europe, a new form of encryption has recently appeared. Called RCE (Regional Code Enhancement), it is designed to stymie freer trade in DVDs. On an RCE-affected disc some DVD machines will display a picture of the globe with a smug announcement that the DVD is designed to play only on Region 1 machines. However, as with all technical patches a number of firms that hack machines to play Region 1 discs will do the same for those affected by RCE. Some DVD retailers will indicate when a disc has been encrypted in this way and recommend avoidance unless you know your machine can play it.

Recordable DVD players

At the time of writing recordable DVDs had just become available. They are expensive but their entry on to the market could mean that the plain old players will fall even further in price.

Further reading
The Which? Guide to Going Digital contains detailed information on both CDs and DVDs.

CHAPTER 6

Clothing

As with all products, there are a number of different reasons why we pay so much more for clothing than consumers in other countries. Essentially, we get fleeced in the UK because a combination of high business costs and restrictive laws make it difficult for retailers to source cheaper goods easily.

Discount retailers in the UK find themselves hemmed in by what seem quite innocuous practices, but combine to stitch the market up. For example, a discount retailer of branded goods wants to sell jeans and sweatshirts. She approaches the official distributor in the UK and explains that she wants to sell the goods at cut-down prices. The distributor refuses to supply them on the basis that the retailer does not meet the right criteria (which are not often spelled out). The retailer still wants to get hold of the goods, so tries to get them outside the country. Within Europe, the prices the retailer is quoted are likely to be lower than in the UK, but not low enough to make importing them worthwhile, and besides the brand owner may frown upon any supplier outside the UK supplying the discounter. If the retailer then tries to get the same goods cheaply from the USA, Latin America or the Far East she is likely to fall foul of the trademark rules.

In addition, a system of protection called the Multi Fibre Arrangement (due to expire in 2005) means that clothing is more expensive in the UK. This essentially limits imports of textiles from developing countries (very often the most important sector for such countries) to protect inefficient

European producers. It has jacked up prices for European consumers and left a legacy of high-cost clothing products.

Cutting the cost

There are a number of ways of getting around the problem of expensive clothing.

Branded *vs* non-branded goods

The first thing to do is to work out whether you are looking at branded or non-branded goods. For branded goods – those bearing the name of the manufacturer, which may include unknown makers in addition to famous or designer labels – the UK is certainly 'treasure island'. Comparison with prices in the USA indicates the degree to which we are getting a raw deal from the brand owners.

There are few genuinely non-branded goods. When the Japanese retailer Muji entered the UK it sold itself as a no-brand retailer – and indeed the clothes and products that are sold are not branded in an ostentatious way. However, Muji itself has become a high-street brand in its own right. Hot on the heels of Muji's success another Japanese retailer, Uniqlo (**www.uniqlo.co.uk**), has recently entered the UK market. Asda (☎ (0500) 100055, **www.asda.co.uk**) has been operating a pretty successful non-brand brand in George for some time. Prices for brands like George and other discount operators like Primark (**www.primark.co.uk**) and Ethel Austin (a chain of discount stores with no website) tend to be not much higher than for similar goods in the USA and Europe.

The domestic discount sector

There has been high growth in what is broadly called discount retailing in the last few years. This sector ranges from firms you will have heard of to less well-known companies, and embraces a wide range of sources. There are essentially two categories of discount retail operation in the UK: the all-in-one discount store and the discount 'village' which contains several shops and may sprawl over a large site. One-off operators are also players, such as Tesco (☎ (0800) 505555, **www.tesco.com**) and Asda (☎ (0500) 100055, **www.asda.co.uk**).

Where the goods come from

What you'd find on sale in discount retailers are all legitimate goods that are made by the firms whose name appears on the label. There is often a suspicion that the sort of items you see on the shelves of discounters are in some way dubious. In the past there was a problem with small stalls selling knock-off or counterfeit goods. However, the big firms operating in this sector are very careful about their supply lines and some have good relationships with the brands themselves. Indeed, in many of the discount villages the brand-owning firms sell direct to the public.

The goods in discount stores come from a variety of sources. The most common sources are:

- misreading of the market
- production over-runs
- past-season or poor-selling stock.

Misreading the market is easy to do and costly for brand owners – this is truer now than ever before as product cycles are down to weeks, rather than months. It means that discount retailers with well-placed buyers can snap up large amounts of current season stocks at significantly lower prices.

Production over-runs occur when a firm produces a fixed volume of stock and then finds that it has too much on its hands. This can happen during a recession or when the firm suffers a sales slump (for example, if jeans become unfashionable).

Past-season or poor-selling stock is another obvious problem for brand owners. If the country has a particularly warm winter, or cold summer, a brand owner can be faced with a huge amount of stock from the last season and nowhere to shift it. Similarly, a brand owner can simply make a line of products that sell poorly.

The established discounters prefer the over-run and over-stock route and many have formed solid relationships with brands that regularly suffer such problems.

Other sources, less common than the headlines suggest, include the 'grey market' and direct orders from sub-contractors working for the big brands. (The grey market is the import of legitimately made goods without the knowledge or acquiescence of the brand owner.) Similarly, some retailers go directly to the sub-contractor to access large stocks of low-price products excluding the brand owner.

Tips on discount shopping

All shopping choices involve some risk; the discount sector is no exception. There are, however, some risks peculiar to the sector that need to be borne in mind. They should be taken into account when hunting out the bargains.

Check the sizing

Always check the size – or be prepared to pass on to friends! There is no such thing as an internationally accepted size. Differences between US, European and UK sizes often create confusion. As a rule of thumb, check the label given by the store and make sure it is accurate by trying on the garment. Simple human error can lead to a product imported from a country with a different size convention getting the wrong label.

Size comparison charts

Women *Dresses and suits*

UK	6	8	10	12	14	16	18	20
European	34	36	38	40	42	44	46	48
USA	4	6	8	10	12	14	16	18

Men *Suits and overcoats*

European	46	48	50	52	54	56	58
UK/USA	36	38	40	42	44	46	48

Shirts

European	36	37	38	39	41	42	43
UK/USA	14	14½	15	15½	16	16½	17

Children

European (cm)	125	135	150	155	160
UK (ins)	43	48	55	58	60
USA	4	6	8	10	12

Shoes

UK	2	3	4	5	6	7	8	9	10	11	12	13	14	15
US men	–	–	–	6	7	8	9	10	11	12	13	14	15	16
US ladies	4	5	6	7	8	9	10	–	–	–	–	–	–	–
European	34	35.5	36.75	38	39	40.5	42	43	44.25	45.5	47	48	49.5	50.5

Check why a product is there

Do a bit of forensic shopping – check the products as well as
the sizes. Always try to identify the reason why the product is
in stock. If it is a 'second' then it should clearly state so. Some
retailers indicate what the fault is and some don't – in this
case you need to carry out an investigation. Don't panic too
much about quality as many brands are so picky about their
products that it is quite difficult to tell a second from a prime
example.

Consider unknown brands

Don't worry if you come across a brand you don't recognise.
Discount stores can often be good sources of brands that are
not normally available on the UK high street.

Consider the season

Two seasonal problems exist in discount retailing – overstocks tend to come on the market as seasons are ending (i.e.
lots of summer gear appears in stores in the autumn), and last
year's overstocks come on to the market a year late.

Buying clothes out of season is generally best done as a
stocking-up exercise for next year. The second factor has a
gender bias. Womenswear tends to be more cyclical than
menswear – or to put it another way, men's fashion doesn't
change a huge amount (as a general rule men tend to be less
aware and less prone to swings in fashion). This is great news
for men as much of last season's stock tends not to look that
different to this year's stock. This applies more to basics (such
as jeans, T-shirts and underwear etc.) than to high-fashion
items. Women can also find some bargains when shopping
for these sorts of basics.

Be patient

If time is of the essence, don't discount shop – or learn to forage. One of the downsides of discount retailing can be the sheer volume of goods that you have to wade through to find what you are after. Goods tend to be arranged by size (although some brands get special treatment) and are racked in no particular order. Depending on the store, you may find that other customers mix up the sizes, which can be annoying. Perseverance usually pays off but you can sometimes get a bit 'snow blind' from the sheer volume of stock.

Enjoy yourself

Discount shopping is fun if you go into it with the right attitude. All shoppers know that bagging a bargain is a thrill. With discount shopping that bargain might take a little time to hunt out – but it will be there.

Shop till you drop – but don't get carried away

Unless you can afford it, discount shopping is a false economy. Remember you have to pay for items you save money on. Spending £60 to save £150 is not a bargain if you don't have £60.

Where to shop

Shoppers in the UK have the choice of all-in-one discount stores or discount villages.

All-in-one discount stores

The UK has had discount stores for some time, but the arrival of US firms and the growth of home-grown 'clubs' have seen this sector take off.

All-inclusive or department-store discounters sell a wide range of goods from a number of firms. These discounters often have established relationships with some brands and opportunistic sourcing with others. They tend to be the quickest route into discounted branding, and their location makes them more accessible, particularly for those without cars.

The all-in-one discounters operate like a normal department store. All sell clothing, and some sell everything from beds to luggage, household items and toys. Three of the best established stores are TJ Hughes, Matalan and TK Maxx.

TJ Hughes
☎ 0151-207 2600, **www.tjhughes.co.uk**
TJs started as a regional discount player in the north-west of England, but in the last couple of years it has started to move into the Midlands and the south. Store format is traditionally based around a large clothing sector, but unlike some other discounters, TJs has a history of large household goods and bedding sections. In an average store the range of products can be quite large. Clothing ranges can be limited, but this has the advantage of reducing the amount of time needed to browse. TJs also tends to stock more discount cosmetics and bathroom goods than either Matalan or TK Maxx and will often also stock non-branded or low-price niche products, such as non-artist genre music CDs and cassettes.

Matalan
☎ (01695) 554391, **www.matalan.co.uk**
Like TJ Hughes, Matalan has been a longer-term part of the

UK retail market. The group was founded in 1985 and operates as a members-only club. There are over 140 stores nationwide with over six million members. The acquisition of Lee Cooper Jeans products, including the Falmer range, has effectively turned the look of Matalan into a cross between a discounter and Gap.

TK Maxx

☎ (01923) 473000, **www.tkmaxx.com**, **www.tjx.com**

TK Maxx is the European operation of the huge TJX group of discount companies (which includes TJ Maxx, Marshalls, HomeGoods and AJ Wright stores in the USA and Winners stores in Canada). It started operating in the UK in 1994 and now has almost 130 stores. Because of its vast parent company, TK Maxx tends to be able to stock a very broad range of products from both Europe and the USA. This gives it a particular strength in sportswear and children's clothing (including what are normally very expensive US brands, such as OshKosh).

Both menswear and womenswear offer broad choice, with occasional strength in certain brands. Often, relatively esoteric US brands and team merchandise are available (good for the teen market). Upmarket brands can be found, and recent coups have included classic Smedley knitwear.

Store sizes vary. Toy sections can be good, if quirky, and household ornaments and kitchen paraphernalia are a strong point. Regular end-of-season clearouts are held, with even better discounts available on normal discounts.

The best branches tend to be found as 'anchor' sites in retail villages and shopping centres (such as those in Hatfield, Birkenhead and Leeds).

Discount villages

While the all-in-one discount department stores are the well-established face of discount retailing, the more recent and high-profile development in the sector has been the emergence of the discount or 'designer' village. While outlet stores have operated for many years attached to factories (the first one was reportedly sited in France in the 1920s), it is only recently that dedicated versions of the US 'outlet mall' have begun to pop up in the UK.

Discount villages tend to operate away from town centres and cover a large area of land near motorway junctions. They usually operate on principles similar to those seen at airports and offer retailers a relatively low basic rent supplemented by a revenue-sharing scheme with the landlord. Given this commercial similarity, it is not surprising that one of the biggest outlet developers is run as a joint venture by BAA (which owns Heathrow, Gatwick and Stansted) and McArthurGlen. Leases for stores tend to be very short term, so under-performers can be quickly removed, and stipulations may require prices to be 20–40 per cent below the high street. The majority of discount villages have tenants made up of the big labels or franchises that specialise in one brand. The presence of multi-brand discounters (such as TK Maxx) is rare, although the Hatfield Galleria is anchored on a TK Maxx store.

The UK discount village market is close to saturation and by the end of 2002 new openings are less likely. After that it is probable that the mega-malls will start to dominate local areas, such as Cheshire Oaks for Merseyside/Cheshire and North Wales. The most likely evolution after this is evident in Manchester's Lowry Galleria, which at the time of writing is expected to house a hotel, a multiplex cinema, bars, restaurants, an office complex and even luxury flats.

The major centres are listed below.

England

McArthurGlen Designer Outlet, Ashford
Ashford, Kent (☎ (01233) 895900,
  www.mcarthurglen.com)

Bicester Village, Oxfordshire (☎ (01869) 323200

Brighton Marina Village, East Sussex, **www.brighton-
  marina.co.uk** (☎ (01273) 693636)

De Bradelei Wharf, Dover, Kent (☎ (01304) 226616)

Cheshire Oaks, Ellesmere Port, Cheshire
  (☎ 0151-348 5600, **www.mcarthurglen.com**)

Clacton Common, Clacton-on-Sea, Essex
  (☎ (01255) 430777)

Clarks Village, Street, Somerset (☎ (01458) 840222,
  www.realm-ocm.com)

Evesham Country Park, Worcester, Worcestershire
  (☎ (01386) 41661)

Freeport Braintree, Essex (☎ (01376) 348867,
  www.freeportplc.com)

Freeport Castleford, West Yorkshire (☎ (01977) 520153,
  www.freeportplc.com)

Freeport Fleetwood, Lancashire (☎ (01253) 877377,
  www.freeportplc.com)

Freeport Hornsea, East Yorkshire (☎ (01964) 534211,
  www.freeportplc.com)

Freeport Talke, Stoke-on-Trent, Staffordshire
  (☎ (01782) 774113, **www.freeportplc.com**)

The Galleria, Hatfield, Hertfordshire
  (☎ (01707) 278301, **www.factory-outlets.co.uk**)

Great Western, Swindon, Wiltshire (☎ (01793) 507600,
  www.mcarthurglen.com)

Gunwharf Quays, Portsmouth, Hampshire
  (☎ 023-9283 6700, **www.gunwharf-quays.com**)

Jacksons Landing, Hartlepool (☎ (01429) 866989,
   www.jacksonslanding.co.uk)
K Village, Kendal, Cumbria (☎ (01539) 732363,
   www.kvillage.co.uk)
Lightwater Country Shopping Village, Ripon, North
   Yorkshire (**www.lightwatervalley.net**)
Lowry Galleria, Manchester (☎ 0161-848 1848,
   www.the-designer-outlet.co.uk)
Mansfield, Derbyshire (☎ (01773) 545000,
   www.mcarthurglen.com)
Peak Village, Matlock, Derbyshire (☎ (01629) 735326,
   www.peakvillage.co.uk)
Royal Quays, North Shields, Tyne and Wear
   (☎ 0191-296 3743, **www.realm-ocm.com**)
Whiteley Village, Fareham, Hampshire (☎ (01489) 886886,
   www.whiteleyvillage.com)
Wilton Shopping Village, Wiltshire (☎ (01722) 741211)
York (☎ (01904) 682720, **www.mcarthurglen.com**)
Yorkshire Outlet, Doncaster, South Yorkshire
   (☎ (01302) 366444, **www.realm-ocm.com**)

Scotland
City Quay, Dundee (Dundee Tourist Board
   ☎ (01382) 221118)
Freeport Scotland, West Lothian (☎ (01501) 763488,
   www.freeportplc.com)
Gretna Gateway, Dumfries, Dumfries and Galloway
   (☎ (01461) 339100, **www.gretnagateway.com**)
Livingston, West Lothian (☎ (01506) 423600,
   www.mcarthurglen.com)
Loch Lomond Factory Outlets, near Glasgow (☎ (01389)
   710077)
Sterling Mills, Tillicoultry, Clackmannan (☎ (01259)
   752100, **www.sterlingmills.com**)

Wales

Bridgend, South Wales (☎ (01656) 665700,
   www.mcarthurglen.com)
Festival Park, Ebbw Vale, Blaenau Gwent
   (☎ (01495) 350010)

Cutting the cost abroad

We can either kid ourselves that people only shop on
holiday abroad because they are bored or it is raining, or we
can just admit that Brits like to shop wherever they are.
Indeed, the notion that we shop only when we have to has
been exploded by the fact that tour operators now offer
shopping-specific trips to various points in the USA and
Northern France.

There is a considerable amount of good news for UK
shoppers planning a trip abroad. First, prices do tend to be
lower for most clothing – the reasons for which are never
particularly obvious. Second, the long run of a strong pound
at the time of writing means that you can buy even more
foreign goods for your tourist money. Third, if you go to the
USA you can't move for outlet malls and discount stores –
and Europe is catching the discount bug too. In the USA
there are now about 312 factory outlet centres, roughly
three times the number in 1988.

Discounters in Europe

Discount retailers have failed to take off in Europe, for a
number of reasons. One is that certain countries, Germany
being the most extreme, have made it almost impossible to
offer discount goods. Until mid-2001 it was illegal in
Germany to discount goods to a level of about 5 per cent

below the manufacturer's recommended price. In France the number of outlet malls has slowly edged up to about 13, with one next door to Disneyland Paris, while in Spain four outlets are near completion at the time of writing (four years after the first).

The UK and US developers have started to push heavily into the European market, and if you are in the vicinity of any of the following outlets they are worth checking out. For multi-product discounters look for Quai des Marques in France and Fox Town Factory Stores in Switzerland.

France
McArthurGlen Designer Outlet Centre, Roubaix
   (☎ 00 33 32833 3600, **www.mcarthurglen.com**)
McArthurGlen Boutiques de Fabricants, Troyes
   (☎ 00 33 32570 4714, **www.mcarthurglen.com**)
Marques Avenue, Troyes (☎ 00 33 144 54 8400)

Around Paris
Quai des Marques, lle–Saint-Denis (☎ 00 33 144 54 8400)
Quai des Marques, Fraconville (☎ 00 33 144 54 8400)
Usines Center, Villacoublay (☎ 00 33 144 54 8400)

Other European countries
Austria
Parndorf (☎ 00 43 2166 3614,
   www.mcarthurglen.com)

Germany
Zweibrücken fairly centrally located between Frankfurt and
   Stuttgart (☎ 00 49 63 329 9390,
   www.outletcentres.com/zweibruecken.htm)

Italy
Between Milan and Genoa, Serravalle
   (☎ 00 39 0143 609000, **www.mcarthurglen.com**)

The Netherlands
Roermond (☎ 00 31 47 53 51 777,
    www.mcarthurglen.com)

Spain
Las Rozas, near Madrid
(☎ 00 34 91 640 49 00, **www.lasrozasvillage.com**)

Sweden
Arlandastad, near Stockholm (☎ 00 46 85 944 0811,
www.outletcentres.com/arlandastad.htm)
Freeport, Gothenburg (☎ 00 46 300 57 00 50,
    www.freeportplc.com)

Switzerland
Outletpark, Murgenthal
    (☎ 00 41 62 926 3070)

Discounters in the USA

Giving ideas for shopping in the USA is the subject of a book on its own. Here we limit ourselves to some general shopping tips and some specific advice about centres that attract a lot of Brits on holiday, such as New York, Boston, Washington DC, Los Angeles and San Francisco.

To get the best deal, travellers in search of a bargain should follow the tips below on discount shopping.

Take a spare bag

Travel light and return heavy. Even if you do not mean to shop when on holiday in the USA, the chances are that you will. It is better to assume that you will shop in advance and take a spare bag, or travel out light in the first place – the savings you make on clothes can very often be more than the air ticket cost in the first place.

Beware extra tax

Holidaymakers in the USA should remember that the US shelf price is always quoted without tax, unlike UK and European prices which include tax. This is because sales tax is different in every state and is added at the checkout.

Some states have no tax at all (e.g. New Hampshire) or tax on clothes up to a certain value (e.g. New York and Pennsylvania).

Look for large sizes

If you are a little on the large size, the USA is the place for you – more of the population are bigger than average, and unlike European manufacturers, clothing retailers in the USA have cottoned on to this fact. Sizing seems to starts at XL, and you can even find sizes up to 5XL or beyond.

Values may be different

Don't assume that brands have the same position or status in the USA as in the UK. Many niche brands found in the UK and Europe are much more down- or mass-market in the USA which makes them cheaper. In the same way, some well-known UK brands such as Ben Sherman may be unknown or very expensive in the USA. Don't be put off by your perception of pricing at home – or expect to find your favourites.

Similarly, you may come across unfamiliar clothing categories such as workwear – for example, jeans are less likely to be considered as designer wear. One of the joys of US brand shopping is the fact that jeans and related leisurewear tend to be seen as 'ordinary' and thus cheap.

Look for unique brands and street cred clothes

Street cred comes dirt cheap in the States. Hip-hop culture has contributed to the popularity of a number of 'workwear' brands such as Carhartt (**www.carhartt.com**), Dickies (**www.dickies.com**) and Ben Davis (**www.bendavis.com**), which are either not available in the UK, or available only at very high prices. In the USA, prices are still reasonable and teenagers who are determined to have Carhartt and Dickies can bag serious bargains, while Ben Davis tops the 'cool' stakes in their use of the grinning gorilla logo. Other less obvious products are also available – for example, OshKosh (**www.oshkoshbgosh.com**) clothes for adults.

Buying online from the UK

We give the websites of many US retailers below – it may be possible to order clothes from these outlets without leaving the country, although shipping costs may be high. A good online source for workwear is at Siegel's Clothing Superstore (**www.zootsuitstore.com** or **www.bdpants.com**). Siegel's is the only authorised web retailer for Ben Davis that can ship abroad. It also has a natty line in zoot suits.

If ordering in the UK from a US website, bear in mind the sizing advice given on page 77 and be prepared to pay duties, VAT and customs clearance fees.

Do your homework on the web

You can use the websites of international brands such as Gap (**www.gap.com**) and Levi's (**www.levi.com**) to compare US prices with UK prices before you leave home.

Take advantage of the frequent sales

Paying 'full retail' is more difficult than you think. All stores tend to have sales at the 'normal' UK times of the year plus home-grown holidays – namely, post-Christmas sales from 26 December onwards (Boxing Day is not a public holiday in the USA and stores tend to open); end-of-summer sales in July and August; Labor Day sales in early September (these can be impressive); and Thanksgiving Day sales in November (for pre-Christmas goods).

The sales are the best times to hit national chains such as Macy's, JC Penney, Nordstrom, Marshalls and Bloomingdales. It is also a good time to visit the out-of-town general stores like the giant Wal-Mart, the K-Marts and the smaller Target and Caldor. If you are out of town or have a car, a visit to a Wal-Mart is worth it just to marvel at the sheer scale that retailing can reach!

Where to shop in the USA

Shoppers have the choice of general discount stores, dedicated clothing stores and clothing sections of department stores.

Discount stores

As with TK Maxx and TJ Hughes in the UK, a series of stores operate as designer discount department stores in the USA. If you are visiting on a city-only basis these are your best port of call. The sheer number of them precludes a listing. However, they all have websites where you can find out the location of stores and, in some cases, browse online catalogues to see just how cheap the prices are.

Burlington Coat Factory
☎ 001 800 444 2628, **www.coat.com**

A bit of a misnomer, this one – the Burlington Coat Factory is a general discount retailer rather than just a coat store, and is found in a lot of towns and city-centre stores other than Burlington. The layout of these stores can be daunting – the more upmarket stock tends to mean enormous racks of suits and coats that can cause serious giddiness in inexperienced shoppers.

TJ Maxx

☎ 001 800 926 6299, **www.tjx.com**

Very much like their UK cousins, only more so. Stores tend to be larger (and often have different names like Marshalls) and even cheaper. They often specialise in sportswear and casual clothing.

Nordstrom Rack

☎ 001 888 282 6060,
**http:about.nordstrom.com/ourstores/
rackstores/**

Nordstrom Rack is the discount arm of Nordstrom, a very high-quality established retailer. Stock tends to be more upmarket with more exclusive labels, and prices are a bit steeper than in the parent store and other discounters. Very good for formal and smart clothing. If you enjoy the Selfridges sale, then Nordstrom Rack is for you. Remember that each discount store has a sale of its sale stock.

Ross – Dress for Less

☎ 001 800 945 7677, **www.rossstores.com**

City-centre focused stores that are a real treasure trove. They tend to stock merchandise from local sports teams – American football, baseball, basketball, ice hockey etc. – which is an advantage for fans and collectors. For example, sweatshirts for local teams (of all sports) are usually available for under £10. Very good for sportswear and casualwear. Ross also tends to have city-specific merchandise in its stores that will save you a fortune in gifts for relatives (particularly kids).

Department stores and clothing shops

The general department stores such as Macy's and JC Penney have good clothing sections and often stock branded goods as well as their own brand. US-only stores Eddie Bauer (☎ 001 800 625 7935, **www.eddiebauer.com**) and Old Navy (the cheaper arm of Gap – ☎ 001 800 653 6289, **www.oldnavy.com**) offer some bargains.

If you are into hiking, camping or outdoor pursuits and are in the New England area than it is worth heading to an LL Bean outlet store (look up **www.llbean.com** for locations). LL Bean is a formidable catalogue retailer with excellent stock and decent prices. The biggest and best centre in Freeport, Maine, also houses other factory outlet shops.

Discount malls

The USA is the home of the outlet mall, with over 300 spread across the country. The scale of these malls can sometimes beggar belief. Sites like that in Gilroy, California, are actually separate blocks of outlet stores that you have to drive between, while single-site covered malls like the Potomac Mills outside Washington DC (part of the Mills Group chain at **www.millscorp.com**) are simply enormous and require hours to walk around, let alone giving any time for shopping. As a general rule of thumb you should expect to set aside at least half a day to a whole day to be able to check out a single outlet mall. Most, like their UK counterparts, have good food facilities (high availability but a tendency towards fast foods). For more information and location details, check out the sites at **www.outletbound.com** or **www.outletsonline.com**.

Is the regular store cheaper?

Sale racks in some regular stores such as Gap often have clothes at cheaper prices than factory outlet centres, although you may not have such a wide range of sizes and colours to choose from.

Regional shopping centres in the USA

These locations are popular holiday and shopping destinations for Brits. Below is a brief guide to the bargains to be had. All telephone numbers listed below should be preceded with the code 001 for the USA.

New York

Although native New Yorkers tend to shop out of town for their major bargains, city-based Brits can make do with a decent number of discount department stores. As we went to press, the magnificent Century 21 (☎ 212 227 9092, **www.c21stores.com**) was due to reopen after being damaged in the September 11 attacks in 2001. The centre boasts low prices in the quirky setting of an old bank building.

New York is also blessed with the normal array of discount department stores alongside the usual big-name retailers such as Macy's, and Bloomingdales, and has a very good Burlington Coat Factory near 42nd Street. The Avenue of the Americas has a decent TK Maxx.

For outlet malls most New Yorkers head to Long Island and New Jersey as these are outside New York City limits and do not have any sales tax. Good examples of such malls include the Woodbury Commons Premium Outlets sited at

Harriman in the Central Valley area, about an hour or so north of Manhattan (for more details ☎ 845 928 4000).

The Tanger Factory Outlet Centers I and II are located at Riverhead, about 50 miles from Manhattan near the end of Long Island (for directions ☎ 631 369 2732). Other Long Island outlet malls include the Bellport Outlet Centers I and II (☎ 631 286 4952).

The nearest outlet malls to the city are found in New Jersey, at Secaucus and Flemington. At Secaucus you can visit the Designer Outlet Gallery (☎ 201 866 0560) and the Harmon Cove Outlet Center (☎ 201 348 4780). At Flemington are the Circle Outlet Center (☎ 908 782 4100), the Feed Mill Plaza Factory Outlet Center (☎ 908 788 3816) and the Liberty Village Premium Outlets (☎ 908 782 8550).

California

The sunshine state is not short of places in which to shop. Both Los Angeles and San Francisco are well stocked with the established department store discount malls, with Ross better represented on this coast. San Francisco is well placed for discount shopping for those without a car as there is a distinct 'downtown' and good public transport links to the shopping centres in the outer limits of the city. However, as with all US cities, the biggest and best outlet malls are to be found outside the big cities.

In northern California there are a number of outlet malls around the Bay area of San Francisco, including the imaginatively named Great Mall of the Bay Area (☎ 408 945 4022), the Petaluma Village Premium Outlets (☎ 707 778 9300) and the Freestanding Outlets in San Francisco itself. Further out towards Lake Tahoe (a popular destination for many tourists) are the Factory Stores at the Y (☎ 530 573 5545).

If you are taking a fly-drive holiday to either LA or San Francisco and plan to drive between the two, an outlet mall of some considerable size can be found between the two cities (on the San Francisco side) at Gilroy Premium Outlets (☎ 408 842 3729). Gilroy claims to be the garlic capital of America – not necessarily something to shout about! So alongside some bargain shopping you can buy plenty of garlic-related memorabilia and cook books. Talking of outlets on routes between major tourist destinations, Barstow, located between Los Angeles and Las Vegas, boasts both a Factory Merchants (☎ 760 253 7342) and Tanger Outlet Center (☎ 760 253 4813).

Southern California has more than its fair share of outlet malls. Most of the outlet malls around LA are some way out, including Camarillo Premium Outlets (☎ 805 445 8520), the Lake Arrowhead Village (☎ 909 337 2533), and Prime Outlets at the exotically named Lake Elsinore (☎ 909 245 4989).

Boston

Boston appeals both to non-discount shoppers and the discount-hungry, with quite an array of traditional downtown shopping offers. The famous Filene's Basement bargain store (☎ 617 542 2011, **www.filenesbasement.com**) now has branches in New York and elsewhere. The big malls lie outside the city, including the almost obligatory Tanger Outlet Center (☎ 207 439 6822), the VF Factory Outlet Mall (☎ 508 998 3311) and Worcester Common Outlets (☎ 508 798 2581). Those heading for the beauty of a Cape Cod holiday can also check out the Cape Cod Factory Outlet Mall at Sagamore (☎ 508 888 8417).

Florida

The growth in UK tourist visitors to Florida has contributed
a good deal to awareness among UK shoppers about the
high prices that are charged at home. This 'Florida effect' has
been boosted by the presence of a quite dizzying array of
outlet malls clustered around major tourist haunts. In and
around Orlando alone (home of Disneyworld) you can visit
at least five outlet malls. These include the Belz Designer and
Factory Outlet Centres (respectively ☎ 407 354 0126 and
☎ 407 352 3545), Orlando Premium Outlets (☎ 407 238
7787) and the Lake Buena Vista Factory Stores (☎ 407 238
9301).

Other major tourist destinations with outlet malls
attached include Fort Myers with Tanger Factory Stores
Sanibel (☎ 941 454 1974), Fort Lauderdale's massive
Sawgrass Mills (☎ 954 846 2300), Kissimmee
Manufacturer's Outlet Mall (407 396 8900), Prime Outlets
at Naples (☎ 941 775 8083), Sarasota Outlet Center (☎
941 359 2050), and St Augustine with an Outlet Center
(☎ 904 825 1555) and another Belz Factory Outlet World
(☎ 904 826 1311). Vero Beach boasts a Prime Outlets (☎
561 770 6171) and West Palm Beach has an Uptown
Downtown Outlet Mall (☎ 561 684 5700).

Unfortunately you are unlikely to be able to blame the
weather for forcing you into the shopping malls – although
the air-conditioning might appeal if you want to escape the
heat.

Washington DC

Washington DC is hardly a shopper's paradise, with most
malls within the city boundaries being pretty pricey (by US
standards). However, if you get bored with the sightseeing
and have access to a car there are two destinations to check

out. The City Place Mall (☎ 301 589 1091), relatively near the city centre, has a number of the established outlet department stores such as Ross and Nordstrom Rack. Further afield and catering for the huge commuting traffic that lives in Virginia is the Potomac Mills Mall (☎ 703 490 1440), a real humdinger of a discount mall. It has a mix of discount and full-price shops and is absolutely vast. However, to get there you really do need a car, otherwise you will have to shell out for long and pricey cab journey (only worth doing with a large group).

Duty to declare

If you spend over £145 abroad outside the EU on any goods, you are obliged to declare your purchases when returning to the UK and will have to pay tax and duty on the full amount. To help keep track of your spending you should keep the receipts for all the clothing you buy.

Further reading

For more information about buying online, read *The Which? Guide to Shopping on the Internet.*

CHAPTER 7

Computers

The home computer market has grown enormously in the last decade – today 44 per cent of UK households have a computer, compared to 17 per cent in 1990. What you get for your money when you buy a computer can vary enormously, depending on where and how you buy.

From the outside one computer looks very much like another. So why are some so much more expensive than others? And how can you find one that matches your needs? Several factors influence the selling price of a computer. Some, such as performance, can be measured objectively. Others, such as brand image, offer more elusive benefits.

Work out what you want

To get the most from a computer you need to remember that you are buying not just a collection of gadgets and widgets but a complete system – something that is very much greater than the sum of its parts. Computer advertising often tries to lure novice users into spending more than they need by tempting them with promises of speed and power. In practice, these have little to do with long-term usefulness and reliability. Buying a super-fast computer is a waste of time and money if you are going to spend all your time wrestling with it. The first and most obvious thing to do is work out what you want from a computer. You need to ask yourself two basic questions:

- What will I be using it for?
- Will I be the only user of the machine?

The answers will help to determine what sort of machine you need. If you are buying the computer for yourself and are likely to use it for only simple tasks – that is, as a glorified word processor and calculator – then a cheap and basic model may suffice. However, if you will be dealing with large files, especially spreadsheets or databases, a faster machine is more productive. If you plan to edit movies on your computer, play games and surf the Internet – you will need a faster machine with more memory. It is also worth thinking of your future requirements and how easy the computer would be to upgrade.

If you are buying the computer for the family, to give your children access to the Internet (for educational research) and to play games on, you will need a faster machine with more memory and a 3D graphics card.

Whatever your answers to the two basic questions you could save yourself some grief by following these four steps:

1) **Learn the basics** At the very least it's useful to know what the advertising and salespeople are talking about, to be able to compare different processor chips and memory sizes, to know what Windows is and to under-stand what a hard disk does. For more details see the book list on page 106.

2) **Always get a package price** It is reasonable to expect a computer system nowadays to include a printer and multimedia features. If any free software comes with the package, always check it carefully to see how useful it is. A word of caution here, however, you may end up being lumbered with lots of bits you don't want or need or

that is bottom of the range. (*Computing Which?* January 2002 tested some of the printers included in packages and found this to be the case.) You are buying the package for the computer so make that your core concern.

3) **Shop around** Some high-street stores sell systems at an astonishing mark-up compared to certain smaller retailers. You can compare prices in several computer magazines. Cheaper is not necessarily better. Consider after-sales support and location (if you have to take the computer back) as well as price.

4) **After-sales support** This is critical. Customers can learn a lot about a retailer's approach to support from the helpfulness of the sales staff. In a *Which?* report in November 2001, John Lewis provided the best retailer after-sales support, and Dan, Apple and Dell the best manufacturer's support.

Tip

If you buy separate components check that you have the right cables. They can add to the cost.

The computer market

Essentially, there are two overlapping computer markets – one on the high street and in out-of-town retail parks, where brands are centrally important and where 'bundled' groups of products are marketed; and the online market, where more experienced consumers shop and where brands tend to be less well known.

Stocking and warehousing practices tend to mean that high-street and out-of-town stores discount their stock over time. This is worth bearing in mind when innovations (such as new processors and the like) in computing are launched. Online retailers generally divide into the older, established firms, such as Dell, which tend to offer stand-alone products with upgrades available at a discount, and newer entrants, such as Time (now merged with Tiny), which replicate the bundling practices of the offline retail stores more closely.

High street is pricier but good for bundles

High-street computer retailers tend to focus on selling 'bundles' of products to first-time buyers – so rather than offering stand-alone machines they will offer machines packaged with, for example, a scanner, digital camera and printer. This can work out well, but it is rare to be able to negotiate a discount if you don't want all the added extras. See the word of warning about package prices above and remember that you are buying the computer first and foremost.

Online is better value

Online computer firms tend to offer better value for money for the computer itself. They usually operate at set price points (e.g. £599, £999 or £1,299) but rather than just selling the same machine month after month, they continually upgrade the models, so that a £999 machine one year will be a lot better than the one a year earlier. Such firms operate on a 'just-in-time' principle – making computers to order and continually getting in fresh stocks of parts. This 'build to order' policy means that for your money you will get the best machine. However, it also means that discounts are unlikely and that getting an older machine at a lower cost is out of the question.

Apple Macs

The Apple Mac offers a number of important advantages for absolute beginners. It is easier to set up. In a *Which?* survey of November 2001 people found the Apple desktops the easiest of all the computers reviewed to set up. This can help to build confidence with the nervous user. It looks good, works well and is built to a high standard. In the same survey, 79 per cent of Apple users said they would recommend the brand to a friend.

Sometimes second-best is top value

In fast-moving technology markets such as the PC and peripheral market, the speed of innovation can work in your favour. For example, when a new chip is launched (e.g. the Pentium II), the previous version (i.e. the Pentium I) suddenly becomes a lot cheaper. As mentioned above, high-street and out-of-town retailers are often good places to start when looking for discounted and slightly out of date stock. Morgan Computers (see 'Useful contacts') specialise in bringing older stock to the market and selling it at big discounts. If you are after a cheap, slightly less sophisticated machine, then this is the place to start.

Get upgrade components when you buy

If you are buying a PC from one of the big direct or online retailers (such as Dell) you are likely to be offered relatively low-priced upgrades on key components of the PC. For example, you can often upgrade to a bigger monitor for

£150. This is a lot cheaper than having to buy a bigger monitor later on. The same goes for memory and hard drives. If you can afford to, it is worth upgrading your machine on these key items.

Do your research

The shelves of every newsagent in the UK groan under the weight of computer magazines. All carry advertisements and some even index the advertisers, which is very handy. Looking through the adverts will give you a good indication of the sort of stock that is available. If an index is provided, look for any one magazine that has adverts from companies such as Dan, Evesham, Dell and Morgan Computers. (In a *Which?* survey in November 2001 two-thirds of Dan owners were fairly or very satisfied with the technical support overall.) If all of these companies feature as advertisers then a reliable set of benchmark prices can be found.

Know your specification and your price

You need to have two key pieces of information in mind when you go to look at a computer – price and specification. Once you have worked out what you want your computer to do for you, you can draw up an ideal specification for the machine that will deliver that performance. At the same time, you need to have an idea about how much you want to spend. Combining these two criteria will give you an idea of how realistic you are being. If you are lucky enough to marry up your demands with your budget then you can simply look for the best deal. If not, then you need to think about simplifying your specification (for example, perhaps downgrading a graphics card) or digging further into your pocket.

After-sales support

For both the professional and the beginner reliability and after-sales support are important factors to take into account when buying a PC. Always check the cost of after-sales support and for how long it is offered. Also check the latest *Which?* reports of computer reliability. (If you are not a subscriber to *Which?*, or Which? Online, copies should be available in your local library.)

Check for VAT and delivery

One of the most irritating things about PC sales practices is the number of adverts that list the price *without* VAT and delivery clearly added on. Always check that the price you are quoted includes VAT and delivery.

Extended warranties

If you are offered an extended warranty on your computer treat it with caution. Always read the small print to check what it does and does not cover (for example, one warranty covered the hard disk but not the monitor!). Remember, too that it is always worth checking the manufacturer's warranty – it may provide three years' cover on the monitor so there would be no need to take out an extended warranty as well.

Small isn't always beautiful

Laptops are a major boon for busy business travellers and for the space-conscious. They are convenient and stylish – but unless you need the portability you still get less power for your money, more limited display and a less convenient mouse device; in addition to which, upgradability can be limited. So before opting for a portable rather than a desktop computer, consider whether you really need the portability.

Useful contacts

Apple ☎ (0800) 039 1010, **www.apple.com/uk**

Dan ☎ 020-8830 1100, **www.dan.co.uk**

Dell ☎ (0870) 152 4699, **www.dell.co.uk**

Evesham ☎ (0870) 160 9700, **www.evesham.com**

John Lewis ☎ (08456) 049049 **www.johnlewis.com**

Morgan Computers ☎ 020-8575 0055,
    www.morgancomputers.co.uk

Time ☎ (0870) 830 3116, **www.timecomputers.com**

Further reading

For more detailed information about buying a computer and deciding on the best specification for your needs, consult the following.

The Which? Guide to Computers
The Which? Computer Troubleshooter
The Which? Guide to Going Digital
The Which? Guide to the Internet
Computing Which? magazine.

For a full list of Which? Books titles, see the back of the book.

CHAPTER 8

Credit cards

When credit cards were first introduced to the UK, the choice was pretty much limited to Access or Barclaycard. Today, however, the situation is very different. A huge variety of credit-card issuers – from banks to building societies, charities to petrol companies, and even car manufacturers – are getting in on the act. Despite this enormous increase in the number of credit-card providers, however, the majority of UK consumers have proved remarkably unwilling to ditch their expensive cards for much cheaper alternatives.

The boom in the number of providers is reflected in the amount that UK consumers now spend on their cards – card holders spend well over £8 billion each year. But many of those borrowers are paying over the odds for credit. The National Association of Citizens Advice Bureaux estimates that we are paying £4 billion a year too much for credit partly as a result of the games that issuers play in order to increase their profits. These include reducing minimum payments on cards – which can encourage people not to pay off debt and lead to much higher final bills – and offering repayment 'holidays' – which allow interest to accrue and add to the cost of the loan.

Cutting the cost

There are essentially two ways of looking at a credit card: as a tool that will help you save money, or as a flexible way of borrowing money when you need to smooth over dips in your finances.

If you take the first view, you should use the card as a substitute for your current account card, choose one with no annual fee, and pay off the bill in full each month. That will cost you nothing and might even save you money if the timing's right. For instance, you might stop your current account going overdrawn or you might have more money in your current account earning interest while you await your credit-card bill.

If you use your card as a way of borrowing, however, you can be easy prey for the card issuers and need to give careful thought to choosing the most appropriate card for your payment pattern.

What to look for

The first thing to look for when choosing a credit card is that it does not charge an annual fee. There are plenty of such cards and they often have the added advantage of the best rates of interest on borrowing.

What you look for next will depend on how you propose to pay the bill and what you intend to use the card for. There are essentially five main types of card holder, and their payment patterns are as follows.

- **Always pay the bill in full** If you always pay your bill in full every month and never use your card to withdraw cash, you should look for a card with a generous interest-free period (up to 59 days) and choose the perks that attract you (such as air miles, free gifts or new car discounts).
- **Always pay the bill in full but withdraw cash** If you always pay your bill in full every month but use your card

to get cash, look for all of the above features and also for a card that does not charge interest on cash withdrawals if you pay in full. These cards are very rare.

- **Occasionally slip behind in payments** If you intend to pay your bill in full most of the time but sometimes make use of credit, look for a card with low interest and check the method for calculating interest (see overleaf).

- **The constant debtor** If you keep a running debt on your card, you should choose one with a low rate of interest. Because you are the kind of customer that card issuers are particularly interested in, look out for special deals and incentives to transfer your debt from an existing account. The new entrants to the card market – particularly the American issuers such as MBNA, People's Bank and Capital One – thrive on this secondary market in debt.

- **The frequent traveller** If you want to use your card to get foreign currency and/or make purchases abroad, make sure that the card you choose has all the features appropriate to your bill-paying method, plus low exchange-rate loading (a 'conversion fee', which differs between individual card issuers).

Tracking down the right card

You can use the Internet to help you find good deals to suit your individual circumstances. Product-comparison websites such as the ones listed overleaf give you access to extensive databases that are updated daily. Once you have specified your criteria, such as 'lowest standard interest rate' and 'no annual fee', the database will suggest cards that meet your requirements.

Product-comparison websites
www.ftyourmoney.com
www.moneyextra.com
www.moneyfacts.co.uk
www.moneynet.co.uk
www.moneysupermarket.com

Calculating interest

How much interest you pay depends on the interest rate – usually expressed as both a percentage per month and as an annual percentage rate (APR) – and on the method used for calculating the interest charge.

Different providers start and stop charging interest on transactions at different times, so if you have two cards with the same interest rate you could end up paying more interest with one than with another. There are at least six different methods of charging, and they can be complicated (for a more detailed explanation, see *Which?*, November 2001).

If you use your card to borrow (i.e. you do not always pay your bill in full) it is important to understand how the interest is calculated. If you already have a credit card, your monthly statement should show clearly on the back which method is used, and how interest is applied to different transactions. If you are considering opening a new credit-card account (or switching cards), check the provider's terms and conditions to establish which system it uses.

There are various myths regarding the interest that you'll be charged on credit card transactions. Some examples are as follows.

● *If I pay part of my bill I'll only pay interest on the amount outstanding* In reality, if you 'part-pay' you'll pay interest on the full amount that you borrowed.

- *If I pay my bill in full, I won't be charged interest* Generally you won't. But with some cards you will, because they charge you interest from the statement date right up until the day you pay in full.
- *If I pay my bill in full, I won't be charged interest on any new purchases I make in the month I pay in full* Again, generally you won't. But some cards will charge you interest on new purchases – as well as the outstanding amount – unless you've paid off every penny.
- *If I pay my bill off in full, I won't have to pay interest on cash withdrawals* Many cards charge you interest on cash withdrawals from the date you make them until the date you pay in full. If you don't get charged for withdrawals, you might have to pay a handling fee.
- *All cards have an interest-free period* Some cards don't give an interest-free period – and are therefore good for people who continuously have a balance owing. If you normally pay in full, however, avoid these cards.
- *When I make a purchase, all credit cards will start charging interest around the same time* Some cards start charging interest from the date you made the purchase, whereas others charge from the date the transaction reaches your account (this is normally a couple of days after the transaction).

Other charges

Be aware of the possibility of unnecessary and potentially expensive charges that could be incurred from your card issuer. These might include:

- a **late payment charge**, of up to £20, if you fail to make payment by the due date or don't pay the minimum required

- a **returned payment charge**, of about £10, if the cheque you use to pay the bill bounces or the direct debit is returned unpaid
- a **letter charge**, of about £10, if the card issuer has to write to you because you have broken the terms of the agreement
- a charge for **duplicate statements**, of about £5
- a charge for **duplicate vouchers**, of about £5 per copy.

Hidden perks

One of the great benefits of using a credit card is that in certain circumstances you can ask your card issuer to refund you if something goes wrong with a purchase you've made with it. This isn't something that card issuers choose to publicise (for obvious reasons), but it's a valuable perk, probably more so than the 'purchase protection' or 'reward points' often advertised as a benefit of a particular card.

Whenever you use your credit card to pay for something that costs more than £100 and less than £30,000, Section 75 of the Consumer Credit Act makes the card issuer jointly liable with whomever you're paying if something goes wrong. This can be very useful if you've got a problem with an item you bought and you can't get the retailer to resolve it, or if you've paid in advance for a product or service you don't receive – for example, because the company has gone bust. See also Chapter 19, 'Shopping rights.'

Should I switch cards?

You should definitely switch your credit card if you're paying an annual fee – especially if you always pay your bill in full every month. It can also pay to switch if you use your card to get cash or for holiday spending, and your current card doesn't offer a good deal on these kinds of transaction.

If you use your card to borrow – either occasionally or all the time – you will certainly save money if you can find a card charging a lower rate of interest.

If you run up a debt on your existing credit card, look into the special introductory offers – which typically last for six months to a year – that many card issuers offer. Unsurprisingly, card issuers like customers who pay interest and so are usually very keen to get you to transfer your debt to them. Some offer better rates to people who close down their old credit-card accounts as soon as the switch is made.

If you are thinking about switching – and you should! – you need to ask yourself a number of key questions. These are:

- What will the interest rate be?
- When does the special offer period come to an end?
- How much of my balance will the special low-interest rate apply to? (It may be only to the balance that you transfer and not to any new purchase you make with the card, although you can find cards that apply the low rate to all transactions.)
- Will the transferred balance be treated as a purchase or as a cash advance? (If the latter, the interest rate will be higher.)
- How will my repayments be used? (Most card issuers use your repayments to pay off your transferred balance first.)

There is nothing to stop you switching cards again any number of times, when the special-offer rate on each card comes to an end. However, be wary of cutting up an old card or transferring your balance to a new card until you know what your credit limit is going to be.

The credit limit is perhaps the least-discussed but most important issue for constant debtors. Because of data protection laws it is often difficult for new entrants to the credit-card market to get accurate information about you as a customer. They resort to models of behaviour and credit-worthiness, and information that other firms have about you that is available to credit-scoring agencies. Your current credit-card provider will be able to offer you a much higher credit limit than someone else – whether a new entrant to the market or not – as credit limit is based on your history and the profile information that the company has about you. The longer you are with someone the higher the credit limit you are likely to get. This is worth bearing in mind, since it means that if, for example, you have a credit-card debt of £8,000 and are enticed to a lower-rate card, but it only has a £4,000 limit, then you will not be able to transfer the balance.

Diminish your debt

If you have decided to clear your credit-card debt, it could make sense to become a 'full payer' on your current card by transferring your existing balance to a new lower-charging card – even one that doesn't give free credit. You'll be able to pay off the debt gradually but at a much lower rate of interest – while not incurring interest on your old card.

Store cards

Be wary of using store cards – credit cards that can be used to make purchases only in a certain store or group of stores. Store salespeople often encourage shoppers to make applications with the incentive of instant credit on goods that they're about to buy. Use of these cards is attractive to the stores because they can retain customers and gain an idea of shoppers' purchasing patterns. Customers are attracted by the immediacy of the credit deal and by the perceived kudos of shopping 'on account'. Store cards are fine if they offer perks (such as money-off vouchers) and if you pay off your bill in full each month. However, they can be a very expensive way to borrow and the interest rate can be double that of some credit cards.

Further reading

The Which? Guide to Money. Check *Which?* for recommendations on the best credit cards. The personal finance pages of the weekend press publish weekly Best Buys, usually provided by Moneyfacts (**www.moneyfacts.co.uk**).

CHAPTER 9

Current accounts

Most people need a current account – if you have a regular income and financial commitments, it is difficult to manage without one. It might be an account with a traditional high-street bank or one with some other financial services provider such as a building society, supermarket or Internet bank. Current accounts vary, but most offer a cheque book, payment and cash cards, the chance to pay money by direct debit or standing order, and the option of an overdraft facility.

Despite the arrival of newer competitors, the 'Big Four' – Barclays, HSBC, Lloyds TSB and NatWest – still dominate the market. Banks know that, owing to loyalty or inertia, many customers stick with the same bank for life, after opening an account when they go to college or get their first job. You too may feel like staying with your present bank if it has been reasonably helpful and efficient in the past, or you may think that changing to another bank would be a lot of hassle. It is because many people feel this way that some banks get away with paying pitifully small rates of interest on credit balances in current accounts, or charging for things that other current-account providers offer for free. But switching from an expensive current account to a cheaper one could save you over £100 a year. And switching accounts needn't be stressful if you go about it in an organised way.

Another way in which banks may not be offering you the best deal is in trying to sell you new-style accounts with fancy names, which come packaged with other perks or 'benefits', such as preferential overdraft rates, 'prestige' credit cards or special deals on insurance. These accounts generally cost you a few pounds a month even if you are in credit, and they can work out as poor value unless you really need all the parts of the package on offer.

The real cost of a current account

It is fairly easy to find a current account that costs you nothing provided you keep it in credit. But you are likely to be charged by your bank in any of the following situations.

- **If you go overdrawn** If you do this without your bank's agreement this will cost you more than an 'authorised' overdraft – one that you have arranged before you make use of it. You are also likely to be charged for bounced cheques or letters warning you about borrowing without permission. How much an authorised overdraft will cost you depends on whether, in addition to interest on the amount you borrow, you have to pay an overdraft arrangement fee, a monthly fee or transaction charges. These charges used to be common, but none of the large high-street banks make them now (although they may charge for arranging a very big overdraft). You are more likely to find these charges with the smaller banks, and they are also still usual in Northern Ireland.

- **If your 'cleared' balance goes into the red** When you pay a cheque into your account, the money may not be actually available for you to use until the cheque has cleared (i.e. until your bank has received the money from the other bank). Cheques usually take three to four working days to clear. If your balance falls below zero because you withdraw money before a cheque has cleared, you may have to pay interest and possibly other charges as well. It can be easy to fall into this trap because some banks' cash machine balances, or mini-statements, show cheques credited to your account on the day you pay them in, rather than the day the money actually reaches your account.

- **If you use services for which your bank makes a charge** (such as speeded-up cheque clearance or stopping a cheque).

A few years ago several of the big banks charged (or planned to charge) non-customers who used their cash machines (or customers who used another bank's cash machine) about £1.50 a withdrawal, but now you're only likely to be charged if you use an ATM abroad, or in a 'convenience' location like a shop. The ATM screen should warn you if you will be charged for a transaction.

If you choose a 'packaged' account (see opposite) you will also have to pay a monthly fee even if you stay in credit.

Some current accounts pay next to no interest on credit balances – as little as 0.1 per cent in some cases – so in such cases you are effectively losing money, because better rates are obtainable (see 'Choosing a better current account', see page 124).

Electronic banking

As well as those banks which started out as telephone banks, such as First Direct, most high-street banks now offer a tele-phone banking service that lets you do many of the things you could do by visiting a branch – checking statements, transferring money, paying bills, etc. Most telephone banking services are open for longer hours than branches – 24 hours a day in many cases.

Many banks also offer banking services via your computer or digital TV. You can do this either through the Internet or via a direct link to your bank, for which you will need special software from the bank. Internet banking in particular means you can operate your account from almost anywhere in the world.

As well as the Internet banking facilities offered by high-street and telephone banks, there are also a few Internet-only banks, such as Cahoot, Intelligent Finance and Smile, offering current accounts (you may still get physical cheque books and cards, but don't get paper statements sent to you). First Direct also offers an Internet-only account. There is also the option – though it is still early days – of using a mobile phone to access the Internet for banking on the move.

You may find it efficient and convenient to deal with your finances without queuing and at a time and place that suit you. Most Internet-only accounts also pay rather better rates of interest on credit balances than traditional branch-based current accounts do. But it also suits the banks for you to do your own banking: it costs them less to run these electronic services than to maintain and staff high-street branches. Remember too that if you do not select an Internet Service Provider (ISP) that provides unmetered Internet access, the cost of dealing with your account online can mount up.

Cutting the cost

Everyone has slightly different financial circumstances and you need to think carefully about what sort of current account is best for you. But whatever your banking needs, it pays to review the current account you have. This is especially true for those who bank with the Big Four high-street banks – the current accounts offered by these banks are rarely, if ever, good value for money. There are essentially two ways around the problem of poorly performing current accounts: making your existing account work harder, or changing to a better account.

Making your account work harder

Whichever bank you are with and however willing or reluctant you are to contemplate change, it pays to use your head when using your account. When you review your current account you should bear the following tips in mind.

Beware banks offering packages

Don't be talked into switching to a 'packaged' account that carries a monthly fee unless you are sure it really fits your needs. If you won't need all the elements of the package then you'd be better off buying them separately, as and when you need them. Take a long, hard look at the 'perks' – you may have them already, they may be insufficient for your needs, or you may be paying over the odds for them.

Be proactive with your existing bank

If you have an ordinary current account, your bank might not tell you about other kinds of account which would offer better terms, so it is worth asking about these. An 'all-in-one' account, for example, which can combine a current account with a savings account, credit card and mortgage from the same provider, may be a good deal if you have a mortgage.

Consider virtual banking

If you are happy to do without branch access, Internet-only accounts (see 'Electronic banking', pages 119–20) may well give you a better deal. Many high-street banks offer Internet banking – if you are thinking of switching it might be worth trying out banking online with your existing bank first.

Don't just withdraw cash from any old machine

Find out which ATMs, if any, you'll be charged for using to make cash withdrawals or other transactions.

Assume cheques clear at a snail's pace

If you are relying on using money that has come from a cheque you've recently paid in, check with your bank whether it has cleared before making a withdrawal. Banks can take an age to clear cheques and place the money in your account.

Don't be afraid to peek

Many people feel almost phobic about looking at their bank balance. But keeping a day-to-day check on your account balance, although tedious, reduces the risk of inadvertently going into the red. So also does the practice of keeping an accurate running total of your balance and your own record of all your transactions.

Know your limits

Try not to get overdrawn, or exceed your overdraft limit, without making an arrangement with the bank. Most banks don't charge a fee to arrange an overdraft, but even if yours does, it is still likely to cost you less than going overdrawn without permission. If you want to borrow for a major purchase, other types of loan are generally more suitable than an overdraft (see Chapter 14).

Get a better return on your money

Don't keep more money in your current account than you need to. Many current accounts (especially those offered by the Big Four) pay a derisory amount of interest. Instead, open a high-interest or savings account and transfer money between that and the current account as you need it. Or consider a 'sweeper' account, which automatically transfers sums above a fixed level into a higher-interest savings account (but check if there is a charge for this service). However, be wary of leaving money in a savings account if your current account is regularly overdrawn, as the interest you get will usually be less than what you have to pay on the overdraft.

Be promiscuous with your money

You don't have to show loyalty to your existing bank. There is nothing stopping you opening a second current account with a different bank – for example, using the one with the best overdraft terms for paying your bills from, if you expect to go into the red, and the other for cash withdrawals.

Use a fine-tooth comb on your statements

Check your statements carefully for errors and if you find a problem ask your bank to explain and, if necessary, to put matters right (see 'The Banking Code' on pages 128–30). If your bank makes a mistake that causes you to go overdrawn, it should pay back any charges or other deductions taken from your account as a result of the error.

Choosing a better current account

If you have reviewed your existing account and found it wanting (and three-quarters of you probably will!) you have the option of moving your business somewhere else. You should not be put off by horror stories of mistakes, errors, delays and rudeness from some years ago: the process now is a lot more straightforward and automated than before. In January 2002, a *Which?* report showed that three-quarters of people who switched found it easy. And it should get even easier now since a new system of automatically switching direct debits was introduced in 2001.

Many people choose a bank because it has branches or ATMs that are handy for where they live, shop or work. If you use a bank's telephone or computer-based banking service then having a local branch may be less important, but you will still need access to convenient ATMs.

You also need to look in detail at what different banks will charge for running your current account. This in turn will depend on whether you are nearly always in credit or, if not, how big your overdrafts are and for how long you tend to be overdrawn. (Don't be put off switching if you're in the red – banks make money from your borrowing so will usually match your existing overdraft limit.) *Which?* reports regularly compare accounts from the Big Four banks and other smaller providers, looking at charges and interest rates as well as how satisfied their customers are with the service they get (if you are not a subscriber to *Which?* or Which? Online, copies should be available in your local library). It is now fairly easy to find an account that pays a reasonable rate of interest if you are in credit, and many offer a fee-free overdraft with reasonably low interest rates.

What to look for

There are a number of questions that you should ask when comparing your account with a rival one.

- **How 'free' is the account?** Is there a monthly fee to run the account? Remember the point about avoiding unwanted packaged accounts. You should avoid any account that isn't free when you stay in credit.

- **Will you have to change your habits?** Are the ATMs that you normally use in your daily routine free to use with your new bank? Although most banks have now dropped the idea of charging non-customers for using ATMs, it is still worth checking.

- **Is interest paid on the money you keep in the account?** You need to find out whether any money that you keep in your account would earn interest and what the interest rate is.

- **What strings are attached?** In order to open the account do you have to keep a minimum credit balance or have your monthly income paid in? This can be the case with some banks that offer good rates.

- **What is the cost of slipping into the red?** Find out how big your overdraft can be before you start paying interest. Some accounts have a small 'buffer zone' of, say, £100 – so you can go into the red by this much during the month before you start to pay anything. You should also find out:
  - the overdraft interest rate (this is likely to be higher with the traditional high-street banks)
  - if the overdraft interest rate is low, whether there is a trade-off between this and a decent credit-balance interest rate

- whether there is an overdraft arrangement fee, a monthly fee, or a transaction charge for every item used when you are overdrawn. These charges are becoming more rare, and it is now much easier to find an interest-only overdraft. In a *Which?* report in October 2001, approximately half of banks surveyed charged overdraft arrangement fees and monthly or quarterly fees, and a quarter made transaction charges.

- **Do you really want the other products the bank may offer you?** When you apply to open a current account the bank may try to sell you other services, such as a credit card, at the same time. Don't agree to anything without taking home the literature and comparing the 'offer' with competing products. A key reason for banks offering current accounts is that these are an 'entry point' to the consumer. The bank will try to use the information it gleans from your current account to sell you different services and products. Be wary of these as they are rarely the best products on the market.

How to leave your bank

Once you have reviewed your existing account and compared it with a few rivals, you may decide that it is time to move your account. Comparing alternative current-account providers using the guidelines above will help you to decide whether it's worth switching, and where to switch to. Switching banks might take a couple of months, but it is not actually as difficult as many people think, provided you plan ahead. The following checklist identifies what you need to do to switch successfully.

- **Make lists** Get a list of all your standing orders, direct debits and regular payments from your current bank, so you can keep track of what money regularly leaves your account and where it goes to. You'll need to keep an eye on the balances in both accounts during the switch.

- **Open your new account ahead of using it** Remember the old adage about changing horses in mid-stream – open your new current account well before you actually start using it. Don't close your old account until the new one is up and running smoothly.

- **Make sure your new bank will handle the switching of regular payments** Until fairly recently, you had to ask each of the organisations you paid by direct debit to send you a new direct debit mandate. But under a new industry-wide system, your new bank should now arrange the switch for you.

- **Tell your employer about the change at the right time** If your salary, pension or benefit is paid monthly, give the payer your new bank details as soon as possible after a monthly payment and ask for the next one to be paid to your new account. Or your new bank may contact the relevant organisation for you if you ask them. If you are paid by cheque or in cash, start paying this into your new account once you have transferred your regular payments from the old bank to the new one. This is probably the most important part of the whole process. The last thing you want is for your bills to be paid out of one account while your pay or pension goes into another!

- **Say goodbye to your old bank** Once you have checked that all payments have been transferred success-fully and your new account is running smoothly, you can close your old one.

The Banking Code

If you have problems with your bank, or if things go wrong, you can refer to the Banking Code to help you. This is a voluntary code which sets minimum standards of good banking practice. Among other things, it commits the bank to:

- act fairly in its dealings with you
- give you information on its products and services in plain language

---

Useful contacts

Major banks

The following are the largest branch or online current-account providers. Contact the customer service line or see their website for more details.

Abbey National ☎ (0800) 731 7774,
www.abbeynational.co.uk

Alliance and Leicester ☎ (0500) 959595,
www.alliance-leicester.co.uk

Bank of Scotland ☎ (0800) 121125,
www.bankofscotland.co.uk

Barclays ☎ (0845) 755 5555, **www.barclays.co.uk**
Co-operative Bank ☎ (08457) 212212,
www.co-operative.co.uk

Halifax ☎ (0845) 720 3040, **www.halifax.co.uk**
HSBC ☎ (0845) 740 4404,
www.hsbc.co.uk

Lloyds TSB ☎ (0845) 072 3333, **www.lloydstsb.com**
Nationwide ☎ (0845) 730 2010, **www.nationwide.co.uk**

- help you choose a product to fit your needs
- keep you informed of interest rate changes
- correct errors and handle complaints speedily.

Your bank should give you a copy of the Code if you ask. You can also get a copy from **www.bankfacts. org.uk**, or also the Banking Code Standards Board (☎ 020-7661 9694, **www.bankingcode.org.uk**). If you think the bank is not putting the Code into practice in the way it handles your

---

NatWest ☎ (0800) 505050, **www.natwest.com**

Northern Rock ☎ 0191-279 4604,
www.northernrock.co.uk

Royal Bank of Scotland ☎ 0131-556 8555,
www.rbs.co.uk

Online-only accounts
www.cahoot.co.uk
www.smile.co.uk
www.if.com
www.firstdirect.com

Product-comparison websites
The following sites recommend a selection of competitive accounts.

www.ftyourmoney.com
www.moneyextra.com
www.moneyfacts.co.uk
www.moneynet.co.uk
www.moneysupermarket.com
www.rate.co.uk

account or the advice it gives you, you can complain to the Financial Ombudsman Service (see below).

If things go wrong

If you have a complaint which you cannot resolve with the firm concerned, contact the Financial Ombudsman Service (☎ (0845) 080 1800, **www. financial-ombudsman.org.uk**). For general advice on how to make a complaint, contact the Financial Services Authority (FSA) (☎ (0845) 606 1234, **www.fsa.gov.uk/ consumer**).

CHAPTER 10

Electrical goods

The market for electrical goods was, until fairly recently, rigged by a number of the manufacturers and retailers to stop decent discounts being passed on to the consumer. The retailers tended to stick to the Recommended Retail Price, or only agreed discounts that the manufacturers were happy about. Thankfully that practice has been knocked on the head by the Competition Commission (or Monopolies and Mergers Commission as it then was).

The legacy of collusion has left the sector rather flaccid and in need of a shake-up. The decision by some supermarkets to enter certain sectors of the market and the arrival of e-commerce have helped to prod the sector into life. However, much of this activity has centred around retailers making comparison shopping difficult and pushing over-priced extended warranties.

Despite the worst abuses of competition being well behind this sector, you need to tread very carefully when buying electrical products.

Before you buy

Before comparing prices, you should consider reliability and energy usage. These factors will make a significant difference to how costly an electrical appliance is to run and could save you money over the long term.

Take reliability into account

Consumers tend to buy things such as fridges and washing machines in the expectation that they will get many years' use out of them. Reliability is a key factor in how long your machine will last and how much it will cost you during its lifetime.

When *Which?* surveyed members about the reliability of their electrical products in July 2000, quite significant differences were seen in the best- and worst-performing products. For example, the most reliable TVs were produced by Toshiba, a record it has held now for six years. Grundig and Thorn tied for the most reliable VCRs. Check the latest reliability tests in *Which?* to find out how these and other electrical goods fare.

Reliability can mean zero repair costs or just an average of a few pounds over a number of years. *Which?* surveys have shown that few appliances require costly repairs in the first five years. Even the most trouble-prone types of electrical appliance – washing machines and washer-dryers – have become more reliable. This makes the expensive extended warranties (see pages 139–40) even worse value for money.

Think green

All 'white goods' that you see on display (fridges, freezers, washing machines etc.) will now display an energy label with a ranking on the basis of energy consumption and performance. The higher the rating the better the performance. If you can aim for an 'A' rating in both, this will not only help you conserve the environment by reducing energy, but it will also reduce your utility bills – making you doubly virtuous.

Keeping tabs on energy usage

As well as looking at *Which?* test reports, you can check out websites such as **www.saveenergy.co.uk** which contain lists of efficient models in the 'white goods' category.

General tips

Before buying, you need to know what features are important for different types of product.

Washing machines

Some top-of-the-range machines tend to have a large number of bells and whistles – don't pay over the odds for lots of features you won't use! However, it has to be noted that cheap machines (under, say, £300) have proved significantly less reliable in *Which?* surveys. What all our surveys show is that there are big variations in reliability among washing machines so it is worth picking a good brand. As we note above, also check the energy efficiency rating for the model and look for economy or quick-wash features, which most machines now have.

Fridges and freezers

Make sure that you get the right-size for your family use. This may seem obvious – but having a fridge that is stuffed to the gunnels will harm the efficiency of the fridge and may lead to food not being stored properly. Having a combined fridge-freezer with separate temperature controls for the two compartments will cost you more up front, but this makes it easier to get the right temperature in each part. Energy labels are important – after all you leave it plugged in all the time – so look for models with a good (A or B) energy label as these will cost less to run. However, past *Which?* test results have found that many energy labels were inaccurate. For example, in February 1997 we found that freezer labels were not accurate, and in October 1998 the same applied to fridge-freezer labels. Reliability appears to be less of an issue for refrigeration appliances.

TVs and VCRs

Once again, go for a reliable brand. Energy-wise, most TVs and VCRs don't use much individually – there's no labelling scheme, but most makers have been following a voluntary agreement to reduce consumption. However, most of us leave TVs, VCRs (and other entertainment electronics) on 'standby' when we're not using them – they usually go to standby when you just switch them 'off' using the remote control – and the electricity used mounts up. One UK survey found that over £160m worth of electricity a year is used by TVs and VCRs doing nothing on standby. So you can do yourself and the environment a favour by switching TVs and other high-tech items off at the mains plug when you can. Check first, though, that clock or station settings won't be lost if power is removed. For product reviews you can look up the website of the Department for the Environment, Food and Rural Affairs on **www.mtprog.com**.

Cutting the cost

You should always shop around to compare prices and get the best deal. As with all purchases, there are some caveats to bear in mind.

Brand names are sometimes not all they seem

Older consumers may prefer makes such as Goodmans, Bush, Ferguson, Hoover and LEC. These used to be prestige British brand names, but are now very average products. It is worth contemplating brands other than those you are familiar with and taking heed of reliability tests, as brand ownership and performance standards can change.

Do your homework

If you have access to the Internet, check whether the equipment you want is available on one of the electrical goods websites. Three of the best are Value Direct (**www.value-direct.co.uk**), QED (**www.qed-UK. com**) and Unbeatable (**www.unbeatable.co.uk**). Phone Value Direct ☎ (01473) 320001 and Unbeatable ☎ (01293) 433833.

Take a leisurely look at the product sector that interests you, then print off the details and price of the machine you like. All three websites say whether the item is in stock or not and give an indication of delivery. The product code should be on the details you have printed off; if not, make a note of it.

Take all this information with you when you visit a retailer and use it as the benchmark. If the product in the store is more expensive (as it is likely to be) you can then decide how much you value taking the product away on the spot, if it is in stock.

It's also worth phoning retailers. Some discount suppliers are available only over the phone, and tend to advertise at the back of magazines such as *Good Housekeeping*.

Get the most from price promises

Many electrical stores make great play of their price promise or price-matching guarantees; some websites feature them too. Many price promises include a refund of a percentage of the difference in price if you find the same item for a cheaper price elsewhere (a 'promise worth pennies'). In order to benefit from a price promise, you have to do your homework first to find a lower price locally and then challenge the store on its promise.

Price promises can be a marketing ploy to convince you that you are getting the best deal and to discourage you from shopping around. They can also lull you into thinking that all shops charge about the same price. But it is worth doing your own research. In December 2001, *Which?* showed that big differences in price exist between high-street stores.

Don't rely on a price promise, and always check the small print and the date of any price comparisons with competitors. You should take price promises with a pinch of salt because:

- prices on the Internet are routinely excluded.
- restrictive conditions will be attached. For example, some price promises require the product to be identical and in stock. This can exclude products that have to be ordered from the manufacturer and are thus never technically in stock
- special editions for shops with different model numbers, or added extras (like a set of additional speakers on a widescreen TV) often mean that the products are not identical. With a bit of study you can usually spot 'different' models which come from the same source but have dissimilar styling and main features

- you may have only seven or 14 days after purchase to challenge the shop with a cheaper price
- the small print may specify how far away the cheaper store can be.

Needless to say, if you go into a shop with a price promise but the price for whatever you are after is not as low as in another shop, don't buy from the shop with the price promise!

Treat sales claims with a pinch of salt

At sale time, remember that signs saying 'up to 50 per cent off' may apply to just a few items, and don't be misled by suggestions of huge discounts. 'Was £x, now £y' claims are controlled by a code of practice, but small print on the sign or in the ad may show that the old higher price was only ever charged at just one branch, for example.

Different stocking policies

Whether you want to compare prices on a specific item or track down the cheapest product in a category, comparison shopping can be quite difficult sometimes because electrical retailers often have very different stocking policies. For example, some chains have their own exclusive brands that are not sold elsewhere. Dixons (**www.dixons.co.uk**) has Matsui, while Asda (**www.asda.co.uk**) stocks products by Schneider, a German retailer, under the Pacific brand. This is not to say that own-brand products are bad value, indeed they tend to offer very keen prices. However, the presence of store-specific brands can make comparison shopping tough.

In addition, getting hold of established brands is not always that simple. Some brands such as Bang & Olufsen (**www.bang-olufsen.com**) have rather limited distribution and comparatively little competition among retailers on price – so you will not find huge savings on items.

Other brands may be more readily available. Big-name brands like Sony (**www.sony.co.uk**) in audio-visual and Miele (☎ (01235) 554455, **www.miele.co.uk**) in washing machines base their appeal on image and reliability. They attract a premium price, but are usually pretty easy to get hold of.

Take delivery times and costs into account

Depending on the product, you either may not be able to take it home with you (because it has to be ordered from the manufacturer) or would not want to (because it is too big and bulky). Take delivery times into account when ordering electrical goods and try to find out the degree to which the shop can be certain of the delivery time. For Internet firms – and outlets for items you order by phone or simply can't take with you – make sure that the delivery cost is included or is clearly indicated. With online retailers you can also take advantage of online order tracking.

Check policy on removal of old equipment

If you want to replace a worn-out fridge or other large appliance with a new one it is probably important to you that the old one be taken away. Make sure that the firm from which you buy has a policy to remove old equipment and find out how much it costs. Otherwise, you will find that you are left with two products and the headache of organising removal. This is important of course for convenience's sake as well as when comparing prices.

If the store you buy from does not remove the old product, it is worth remembering that your local council will offer this service for things like fridges. There can, however, be quite a wait for the council to come and take the thing away.

Steer clear of extended warranties

Extended warranties are schemes to cover you against the cost of repairs on electrical appliances. They are a big earner for many high-street electrical stores, and are a very expensive form of insurance. Sales staff often get commission for selling them and you may be subject to high-pressure selling to buy one. Sometimes, an 'interest-free' credit deal will be available only if you agree to buy the warranty. The cost of a three-year package can very often come to around a third of the price of a product.

However, do you really need this sort of cover? *Which?* has shown that you're much better off running the risk of paying for a repair once the maker's guarantee (usually one year) has run out. For example, on a washing machine, you could pay around £160 for a four-year extension to the one-year guarantee. But a typical washing machine repair costs less than £50 – so the extended warranty would save you money only if your machine broke down more than three times in years two to five – and you stand a good chance of not having to pay anything for repairs at all – regular *Which?* surveys have found that about three-quarters of washing machines don't break down in the first six years.

If you think you need extra cover (and reliability surveys run by *Which?* over a number of years indicate that you probably don't), consider a household 'multi-appliance' insurance policy (from some banks and insurance companies) rather than the insurance offered by the retailer. These policies can be arranged to cover all your electrical goods in one go for a single premium. These are very often a lot cheaper than the single warranties sold by electrical retailers. Alternatively you can seek out a retailer that offers deals on extended warranties. Two of the best in this area at the time of writing are John Lewis (☎ (0845) 604 9049, **www.johnlewis.com**), and Asda (☎ (0500) 100055, **www.asda.co.uk**), which offers a free three-year warranty on all larger electrical goods. In terms of their pricing policy, John Lewis claims to be 'never knowingly undersold' although this does not apply to the Internet.

Interest-free credit deals

Many consumers are lured into buying electrical goods with the promise of interest-free credit. However, caution is needed when taking out these deals. You should check carefully what's on offer; sometimes, to get the interest-free credit you need to take out a poor-value extended warranty. Obviously, if the warranty is over-priced you are not making that much of a saving at all. As always – read the small print. See '0 per cent finance deals' on pages 177–8 for more information.

Own-brand products

The entry by supermarkets such as Asda and Tesco (☎ (0800) 505555, **www.tesco.com**) into the electrical goods arena has spurred a good deal of nervousness amongst general electrical goods suppliers. This is largely because of their success in other areas that were previously closed to them, such as newspapers and magazines, pharmacy products and CDs. Asda tends to concentrate on in-store promotion of its spin-off Pacific brand, and has started supplying DVD players for under £90. This includes additional warranty coverage for three years (offered by Asda on all electrical goods), which removes a good deal of the risk involved in buying a new brand. Tesco has sold widescreen TVs under an Amstrad label and Fujitsu computers. On its website it has a large section devoted to electrical retailing and tends to concentrate on selling well-known brands at a discount.

It is worth contemplating buying electrical goods at a supermarket if you have a loyalty card, as you will gain points on the purchase (see Chapter 15).

Stay informed

Nowadays you do not just buy a product, you buy a complete service. This may mean that, once committed, you are tied into the service. Digital TV and mobile phones are good examples – a retailer may want to sell you a particular product or service and may omit to explain the alternatives. For example, there are three different ways to get the new digital TV channels (terrestrial, satellite and cable). You also have the option of a low-price non-subscription receiver manufactured by Pace (☎ (01274) 532000, **www.pace.co.uk**), but earlier versions did not perform well in *Which?* tests.

Further reading

For more detail see *The Which? Guide to Going Digital*. For a full list of *Which?* Books titles, see the back of the book.

CHAPTER 11

Food

In 1999 the Office of Fair Trading referred the big five supermarkets – Asda, Safeway, Sainsbury, Somerfield and Tesco – to the Competition Commission, but the following year the Commission largely cleared them of the 'rip-off' accusations that had led to this move. By that time, Asda had been taken over by the US supermarket giant Wal-Mart; this triggered a price-cutting war which also went some way towards undermining the earlier charges of profiteering.

Supporters of the large stores say that they've become successful by giving consumers what they want, and surveys confirm that many shoppers are more concerned about quality, choice and convenience than low prices. But all this does not explain the significant food price differences between countries. (On balance most surveys show that the UK is somewhere in the middle of the European league for food prices.) Several reasons have been put forward to justify higher UK prices: exchange rates, different rates of tax, planning restrictions on out-of-town hypermarket developments, and higher fuel and distribution costs. Unlike items such as cars and CDs, knowing that you are paying over the odds for food is not a lot of help as your chances of leaving the country for your weekly shop are slim. Despite the lack of room to manoeuvre, if you know a bit about how food retailers operate you stand a better chance of not spending more than you need on your food shopping.

Cutting the cost

Some people are fortunate enough to have a choice of places to shop for food. Others, perhaps without their own transport and tied to one local store, aren't so lucky. Most people now go to a large supermarket for their main weekly stock-up, perhaps topping up from local shops or delicatessens in between. Recently, more people have also been ordering their groceries over the Internet for home delivery.

There are two main ways you could go about cutting your food shopping bills: changing *where* you do most of your shopping, and then thinking about *how* to save money in the store. But only you can decide how much time and effort you need, or want, to put into saving what may be relatively modest amounts of money at the checkout.

Where to shop

You probably take into account a range of factors in addition to price when deciding where to do the bulk of your food shopping. A *Which?* survey in January 2001 examined how shoppers rate the largest supermarkets on value for money, quality, choice and convenience – this covers a multitude of things under the store's control such as opening hours and waiting times at checkouts. Other factors, such as ease of parking and whether you prefer to go to independent shops for bread, fruit and vegetables or delicatessen items, or to get everything under one roof, also play a significant role in your choice. 'No frills' discount stores such as Kwiksave (part of Somerfield) and chains such as Aldi, Lidl and Netto can work out significantly cheaper than the main supermarkets, though they stock a smaller range of goods and you probably won't find all the things you want or all the brands you are used to or prefer. The *Which?* survey gave the Waitrose chain (mainly concentrated in southern England) the best marks overall, despite it having higher food prices than most.

If price is important to you, you need to be on the lookout for special offers, but on a typical trolley load there aren't huge price differences between the main supermarkets. *Which?* in January 2001 found that you'd typically save less than 10 per cent on a basket of known-brand groceries by switching from the most expensive of the big five supermarkets to the least. Indeed, some supermarkets have been criticised by the Advertising Standards Authority for using short-term price-cuts to make sweeping claims that they were cheaper than a competitor.

The survey found that of the major supermarkets, Asda rated highest for value for money. This is backed up by trade surveys using a basket of popular groceries (both food and non-food items) which have shown Asda most often winning on price over the last few years, followed by Tesco, with Safeway and the more regional chain Morrisons in third place.

Driving a long way to a store for just a few items makes little sense either financially or environmentally, and many people value their small local stores if they still have them.

Once again, the big supermarkets have been accused of using their marketing muscle or political clout to drive small shops out of business. This is a complex issue, but it's fair to say that though small food shops are often more expensive than supermarkets, they aren't necessarily 'ripping you off', as they're unable to negotiate the large wholesale discounts which the big stores can force on their suppliers.

What to buy

It's generally much easier to cut your shopping bills by switching to cheaper brands than by switching super-markets. In particular, check out 'own brands' or 'own labels' – products made specially for a particular supermarket, and sold under their own name or a brand name exclusive to the store. Most stores also have even cheaper 'no frills' ranges of basic commodities such as baked beans or tinned tomatoes (for example, Sainsbury's Economy brand).

In past surveys *Which?* has found that you could save as much as a third on your grocery bill by switching to cheaper brands of the same goods. Taste tests have shown that many own-brand products are of high quality, but as supermarkets are usually secretive about who makes their own-label products, there's no way to be sure without trying them whether you'll like them as much as conventional brands.

Own-label groceries are often prominently displayed on the shelves next to their known-brand equivalents – even the packaging is often remarkably similar. Supermarkets like selling own-label because, though the shelf price is usually lower, they make higher profits on them, and it's also not so easy for shoppers to price-check such items between competing stores.

How supermarkets work

Supermarkets use a range of marketing techniques to get you to go into their store and then buy more things than you'd meant to – the temptingly displayed fruit and vegetables near the entrance, the sweets next to the checkout, the milk located so you have to walk the length of the shop to pick up a quick extra pint. They also put a lot of effort into building customer loyalty so that people don't switch to a different store for their weekly shopping. There's not necessarily anything wrong with all this, but if you know the rules you can play the game on rather more equal terms and be a more informed and canny consumer.

Other marketing tools are linked more directly to price. Perhaps most important of these is what the trade calls the 'known value item' (KVI). Supermarkets have found that shoppers know fairly accurately what a common grocery item such as a pint of milk, a tin of beans or a sliced loaf 'should' cost, and will use this as a measure of how cheap a store seems compared to others. KVIs are often heavily advertised and sold at little or no profit (as so-called 'loss leaders') to get potential customers into the store. But many shoppers don't know the going price for other groceries (and as few stores now put price stickers on packaged goods, when you run out of something you're not reminded what you paid last time), and these goods may be much less competitive. The 'basket' comparisons between supermarkets mentioned above can be a better guide to whether a store is cheaper overall, but only if the range of items in the basket roughly matches what you usually buy. Otherwise, if low prices are a priority, it's mainly down to sharp eyes and a good memory.

Other popular schemes are the BOGOF (Buy One, Get One Free), 'three for the price of two' or '50 per cent extra' type deals. Like other kinds of bulk buying, these can be good value provided you don't overstretch your weekly budget or end up with more short-life food than you can eat or freeze before it's past its best. You might be able to save just as much or more, however, by going for a cheaper brand, and shops sometimes discourage you from spotting this fact by putting a BOGOF deal on soups, for example, at the end of an aisle rather than in the main soups section.

Fresh foods and unit pricing

Stores know that many shoppers are in a hurry or wrestling with fractious toddlers, and you'll almost always pay a premium for convenience: pre-packed fruit, vegetables, meat, fish or cheese usually costs more per kg than the same thing you bag yourself or queue up for at the fresh meat or deli counter. With loose and pre-packaged foods, however, it isn't always easy to be sure you're comparing like with like in terms of quality, freshness or the amount of edible product you get per kg (with or without bone, for instance).

It can also be difficult to be sure which of several items is the best value if they come in different package sizes or weights. Some packaged foods, such as tea, jam, biscuits and cereals can only be sold in certain prescribed weights, which does make price comparison easier. Many supermarkets also facilitate the comparison by using 'unit price' labels on the product or the shelf label to tell you what each item costs per kg or per litre or per 100g serving, for example. Always check these – they will at least ensure that you are aware that you are paying extra for the brand you like.

Problems with price labels

Almost all food stores now use barcodes to enter prices at the till. There are relatively few instances of problems as a result of this method, but they can occur when, for example, a price goes up or down and that price has not been correctly updated on the computer database. In this case the price you're charged may be different from what was marked on the shelf. The shelf price markings themselves may also be unclear and hard to read, especially if certain items are on special offer, leading you to spend more than you intended. Another problem can be checkout staff not knowing which variety of loose fruit and veg you've selected and charging you the wrong price per kg for them. For this reason, it's worth checking your till receipt – shops should always give you a refund if you've been overcharged.

If something is wrongly marked with a lower price, you can't legally insist on buying it at that price. But it's illegal to give misleading price information, or make misleading price comparisons with other stores.

Loyalty cards

'Loyalty' cards were first introduced by Tesco in 1995 as a way of dissuading their customers from switching to other stores. Some other supermarkets followed and loyalty cards have become popular with many shoppers. Typically you get credited with about 1p for every £1 you spend, but this isn't immediately knocked off your bill; what usually happens is that after you've saved up, say, 250 points by spending £250, you get a £2.50 voucher to spend at the store or on other perks. Special offers in-store may attract extra loyalty points. A loyalty card may be combined with a store payment or bank card.

The low rate of return on these cards means they're hardly worth switching stores for, but if you shop at the same store regularly anyway, a loyalty card will save you a few pounds a year (though you may get a stream of junk mail as part of the bargain). For more on loyalty cards, see Chapter 15.

Online food shopping

The early days of Internet shopping were only for the valiant and adventurous. However, most of the super-market sites are now considerably improved, and many big supermarkets now offer Internet shopping with home delivery (at the time of writing Asda, Sainsbury and Tesco from the big five, plus a limited service from Iceland and Waitrose). You may find this method useful if you don't have the time to go to the supermarket or find carrying your shopping difficult, but it's very unlikely to save you any money on your normal grocery shopping (in fact you'll be charged a few pounds extra for delivery in many cases). A *Which?* survey in March 2001 showed that selecting the items you want from long lists on a computer screen is often awkward and time-consuming. And, unless you put in a lot of time and effort, you'll probably end up rather less aware of special offers and how different stores compare on price than you were when you went out for most of your food shopping.

First-time shoppers will find that they need to put an awful lot of effort into doing their first Internet shop, but once that has been done, the next one will be easier. Over time you will find that you tend to repurchase about 80 per cent of the same goods. While delivery costs obviously add to your bill you may also find that impulse purchases are less likely and your kids will find it more difficult to slip items into the basket without you knowing!

Markets and organic food

There's no easy way to know if a street market or farmers' market will be cheaper than a supermarket (in any case, you may choose to shop at markets for the quality of the products or the shopping experience rather than the price). Traditional street markets often sell basic fruit, vegetables and groceries cheaper than competing shops, though unusual items or organic produce are likely to be more expensive wherever you buy them.

Whether organic food is worth the extra money is likely to depend on the importance you attach to the claims made for it, such as improved taste and nutritional value, avoidance of pesticides or better animal welfare. What is important is that you're not misled – the growing demand for organic food and the higher prices it can fetch have increased the likelihood of ordinary produce being labelled as organic, especially where goods are sold loose. If possible, check by asking or looking at the label that the producer or supplier is registered with an approved certification body such as the Soil Association. If you're in doubt about whether food sold as organic is genuine, contact the trading standards office or environmental health officer at your local council.

If you're keen on organic food, it's worth trying the Internet, to see what delivery services are available in your area and how prices compare. But it can still be difficult to compare value for money because the quality may vary considerably from source to source. (See reports in *Which?* February 2000 and August 2001.)

Some organic delivery schemes
www.organicsdirect.co.uk
www.iorganic.co.uk
www.organicdelivery.co.uk
www.freshfood.co.uk
www.absolutorganic.co.uk

The organic delivery market is changing rapidly – to find an up-to-date selection of suppliers, type 'organic' and 'delivery' and 'uk' (or your district or region) into an Internet search engine.

If things go wrong
For advice on foodstore shopping problems, see **www. tradingstandards.gov.uk** or the local council listings in your phone book for trading standards or environmental health departments.

Useful contacts
Customer carelines
Asda   ☎ (0500) 100055
Safeway   ☎ (01622) 712987
Sainsbury   ☎ (0800) 636262
Somerfield   ☎ 0117-935 6669
Tesco   ☎ (0800) 505555

Supermarkets offering Internet delivery
Asda **www.asda.co.uk**
Iceland **www.iceland.co.uk**
Sainsbury **www.sainsburystoyou.com**
Tesco **www.tesco.com**
Waitrose **www.waitrose.com**

Other supermarkets
Aldi **www.aldi-stores.co.uk**
Co-op **www.co-op.co.uk** (and follow link for foodstores via 'our businesses')
Kwiksave **www.kwiksave.co.uk**
Marks and Spencer **www.marksandspencer.com**
Morrisons **www.morrisons.plc.uk**
Netto **www.netto.dk** (and follow link for UK information)
Safeway **www.safeway.co.uk**
Somerfield **www.somerfield.co.uk**

CHAPTER 12

Gas and electricity bills

In previous years who supplied your gas or electricity was not an issue. The local electricity board supplied your electricity and the local gas board your gas. You neither knew, nor really cared a great deal, about the idea of choice in utilities – there was no choice, pure and simple. Since the new market was phased in from 1996, people have been able to shop around for their gas and electricity the same way they shop around for a washing machine or holiday.

The idea behind removing the monopoly from British Gas and the various regional electricity companies was to bring competition to the market and in doing so bring prices down for consumers and drive efficiency up in the companies. As a result there are big savings to be had, but too few people take advantage of them. Many people have stuck with British Gas and their local electricity company, even though they may well be able to save hundreds of pounds a year by switching to another deal. There are three main reasons for this:

- people don't understand how the new system works
- people are afraid of changing to a company they've never heard of, worry it may be a cowboy outfit and fear being left without any power
- they can't work out what the cheapest deal is.

All three reasons are quite understandable: the whole business can be confusing, and trickier to sort out than it should be. But the good news is that, whatever happens, you are very unlikely to be left without a gas or electricity supply.

How it all works

The hard part for many people to get their heads around is that despite the fact that you have moved to a new company, the gas or electricity that you buy is exactly the same stuff as before. Same pipelines and wiring, same physical performance, just a different name on the bill. For example, one company, Transco (which used to be part of British Gas), is responsible for all gas safety and pipework. If you think you have a leak, or some other gas safety problem, you should contact Transco immediately (☎ (0800) 111999), no matter who your gas supplier is. On the other hand, if you have a problem with your electricity supply, you should contact your electricity company.

The part that is different is the supply company – essentially, the cost of bringing the electricity or gas to your house, and billing you for it. Many companies reckon they can do this more cost-effectively than British Gas or the former regional electricity companies, and so they can charge you less for it. Simply put, a newer company can use lower-cost collection techniques and billing systems and pass a share of these savings on to you.

Where to buy

About 20 companies sell gas and electricity in the UK. However, they don't all supply all parts of the country, so you won't have that many companies to choose from.

One of the confusing features is that British Gas now supplies electricity, and most of the electricity companies supply gas, so it's no wonder people have trouble understanding what they're being offered.

You may never have heard of some companies from which you can buy gas or electricity. Many of them are energy companies that have been supplying commercial and industrial users, and have now moved into the domestic (home) market.

You might find you are offered energy from an organisation or association to which you belong. These organisations aren't usually gas or electricity suppliers themselves – they normally have an arrangement with one of the gas or electricity companies, but offer their own tariffs (which might work out cheaper for you than the energy company's 'standard' rates).

Cutting the cost

Even though there is only one type of gas, and one type of electricity, finding the cheapest deal can be harder than it should be. For cheaper gas prices you can check out the Switch with Which site (**www.switchwithwhich.co.uk**). You will find free *Which?* reports and links to price-comparison sites. But always remember that, unlike buying a car or taking out a loan, for example, if you think you've made a mistake, you can always change your mind. You can change suppliers as often as you want. Of course, you will have the inconvenience of having to cancel your contract with the old supplier, and fill in forms to sign up with a new one, but you normally need only give a month's notice to switch companies.

How bills can vary

You might think that, because it's all the same gas and electricity, there's one company which is the cheapest.
Unfortunately, it's not that easy. Some companies are cheaper
for some people than for others, and you need to do some
sums (or get someone to do them for you) before you can
tell who you're going to get the cheapest bills from. That's
because there are several things that will affect how much
you pay.

How much gas or electricity you use

It's pretty obvious that, the more gas or electricity you use,
the more you will pay. But because different companies'
tariffs work in different ways, it's not always straightforward
which will be cheapest. For example, a company with a relatively large standing charge (the amount you pay every
month, regardless of how much gas you use), might have a
low tariff (rate per unit of gas or electricity used); this would
probably mean it is a good deal for someone with a large
family who uses a lot of gas or electricity. On the other hand,
a company with a small – or no – standing charge, but a
higher tariff may work out cheaper for a person living alone,
who uses only small amounts of gas or electricity.

To complicate things further, some companies have
'stepped' tariffs, where you pay different rates, depending on
how much gas you have used each month or each quarter.

Also, for electricity, your bill will depend on whether you
can take advantage of cheap-rate Economy 7 tariffs, which
are offered by all the electricity suppliers.

How you pay your bill

There are three main ways to pay your bill:

- by monthly direct debit
- by a quarterly bill, which you pay on receipt by cheque, card or cash
- with a prepayment meter.

It's cheaper for companies to handle direct debits (and they can be more sure of getting their money on time), so they almost always charge lower rates for people who agree to pay by monthly direct debit. The difference can amount to worthwhile savings (around £20 a year for someone with average gas use). But if you do opt for direct debit payments, you normally pay a fixed amount each month, based on how much the company estimates you will use over a year. This means that you should keep an eye on how much you are actually using (and the estimated usage on bills you receive) to make sure that you are not paying too little or too much, and therefore getting too far ahead or too far behind your bills. If you do get ahead on payments you are essentially giving the company an interest-free loan. If this happens you can get a refund of the money immediately – it is yours after all!

The most expensive way to pay is usually with a prepayment meter, which is unfortunate, since people who have prepayment meters tend to be those with the lowest incomes. So if you have a prepayment meter, you should try and persuade an energy company to allow you to pay by quarterly bill or direct debit. To do this, you may have to pay a deposit equivalent to around six months' worth of gas or electricity.

If you are on benefit, you could use the Fuel Direct scheme, where money is taken directly from your benefits to pay your bills. Find out about this scheme through energy-watch (see 'Doing the sums', pages 159–60).

Where you live

Some companies supply gas or electricity throughout the whole country, but some only sell in some parts of the country. A few even have different rates for different parts of the country, so you may find the cheapest company for you isn't the same as that for a friend or relative who lives somewhere else, even if you use the same amount of gas.

Can you save using the same company for gas and electricity?

Most companies now supply both gas and electricity, and they offer what are called 'dual-fuel' deals. This means that you get a set discount, or pay a lower tariff, if you use the same company for all your energy. It sounds like a great idea, and salespeople often stress the savings by going this route. The fact of the matter is that, although the savings may be worthwhile compared to the normal tariffs, *Which?* found in November 1999 that few energy companies are ever the cheapest for both gas and electricity. Despite the dual fuel discounts, you're probably going to be better off going for the cheapest individual gas and electricity companies.

Finding the best deal

Now that you know the factors that will affect your bills (and what you can do to capitalise on this, whoever you're with), you need to know how to work out which company will be cheapest for you. Finding this information has for some time been an awful lot harder than it should have been.

Treat claims with caution

Many gas and electricity companies have tried to sign up new customers by using door-to-door salespeople and, all too often, these salespeople have confused or misled customers by using exaggerated or simply wrong claims of how much could be saved on bills. Some salespeople have even tricked people into signing contracts that they didn't mean to.

Until the industry cleans up its act, you should treat door-to-door salespeople with caution. Remember, it's simply not possible for them to say that you will save, say 20 per cent or £50 per year on your bills without knowing exactly how much you spend now (see 'Doing the sums', below). Get them to write down exactly how much you will save, or to leave you a leaflet explaining their tariffs so you can work it out yourself, before you sign a contract. Never feel pressured or rushed into making a decision and never sign a document handed to you on the doorstep – always take it and read it at leisure. You won't miss out just because you delay your decision by a week or two, in order to make sure it's the right one.

Doing the sums

To work out which companies offer the best deal, you'll need to do some calculations.

- Get hold of your last year's bills (there should be four of them) and add up your gas or electricity usage, in kWh (kilowatt hours).
- Calculate the gas costs by multiplying the unit rate (pence per kWh) by the amount you use.
- Add on the annual standing charge.

Don't worry if arithmetic isn't your strong point. Some websites can help do the calculations for you – you simply key in your details, and they will come up with your likely bills from all the gas or electricity suppliers in your area, so you can see which would be cheapest. Each of the following work in a slightly different way, but they all provide much the same answer in the end.

www.buy.co.uk
www.saveonyourbills.co.uk
www.ukpower.co.uk
www.unravelit.com
www.uswitch.com

Once you have decided the company you want to sign up with, some companies allow you to register online directly from their website.

If you don't have access to the Internet, or if you'd rather have all the figures in front of you to do your own calculations, the gas and electricity industry watchdog, energywatch, produces a series of factsheets with all the companies' tariffs. They also include calculations for typical household bills, which give you an at-a-glance idea of which company is cheapest in your area. And when you've worked out who you might want to sign up with, they provide contact details for all the companies.

You can get copies sent to you by phoning energywatch on ☎ (0845) 906 0708, or download the factsheets from the energywatch website (**www.energywatch.org.uk**).

Tip

When doing your calcuations, you should take account of all your circumstances (how you want to pay, for example, not just how much gas or electricity you use).

Service vs *price*

Even though the gas or electricity you are getting is the same, whichever supplier you choose, that doesn't mean that all companies are the same. Some companies have a better record for customer service than others – whether it be efficiency, speed in switching from the previous supplier, or how accurate and regular billing and meter-reading is. The consumers' energy watchdog, energywatch, publishes details of each company's service standards, based on the number of complaints people have made about them, on its website (**www.energywatch.org.uk**). You might want to check out how a company is doing before you sign up with a new supplier.

Complaints

If you have a problem with a gas or electricity company, and the company won't sort the problem out for you, complain to energywatch, by phone (☎ (0845) 906 0708, email (enquiry@energywatch.org.uk) or through the website.

Getting the best deal in your region

Not all companies provide gas and electricity in all areas, so if you are making comparisons you need to contact all the right ones. To find the relevant suppliers for your local area, look up the energywatch website or try the tariff calculator sites listed opposite.

CHAPTER 13

Hotel rooms

In this chapter, we look at how to get the most for your money from hotels. For many people the price that they pay for a hotel is totally unknown. If you book a package holiday, the chances are that you will pay one lump sum with hotel costs included. Even if you book a city break or a short holiday all the costs will be included. However, increasing numbers of consumers are now booking holidays in separate chunks. For example, they will buy a trip to Pisa on a no-frills airline and then hunt around for a cheap hotel to stay in.

Cutting the cost

A package holiday is generally the quickest and easiest way to get away, but it may not be the cheapest. Even though holiday companies can get discounts by 'bulk booking' you could still save money by arranging flights, hotels and other items, like car hire, yourself. When *Which?* looked at the cost of a range of short breaks in April 2001, it found that it was generally cheaper to make your own arrangements, rather than go with a package. This applies particularly to mid-range or cheap hotels – if you want to stay in five-star luxury, a package deal may reduce astronomical room rates to something affordable.

And of course, you've got the advantage of a wider choice of flights and hotels, plus more flexibility about when you

want to go and when you come home, if you do all the
booking yourself (see Chapter 1 for details about getting the
best flight deals).

Many hotels do have published room rates (sometimes
the ones you see posted on the back of the room door),
which are known as the 'rack rate'. But these represent the
most you should pay, and how much you actually have to pay
can vary, depending on supply and demand. If you're travelling at a busy time, when hotels have no trouble filling
rooms, you're likely to pay more. Travel off-season and off-
peak, and you should pay a lot less.

The most expensive times depend on where you are
travelling. Fairly obviously, summer is high season for
many holiday destinations (except for winter sports ones,
of course) – although summer prices may be lower if the
local climate is extreme (for example, Florida or Seville).
Places which have a lot of business travellers (European
capital cities, for example) are often cheaper at weekends,
because during the week hotels are full of business people.
And watch out for local events and festivals (such as
Munich's Oktoberfest, or the Edinburgh Festival) when
hotel rooms can be not just more expensive, but impossible
to find.

Exactly how much rates can vary will depend on the type
of hotel. A small guesthouse for example, may have only two
rates: summer and winter. But many hotel chains have very
fluid rates: they price their rooms much the same way
airlines price their seats. They match supply and demand
very precisely, which means that you might get the best deal
by booking a long way ahead – or maybe at the last minute.
Many hotels in the USA are unable to give prices out for six
months ahead.

Where to buy

There are various ways to find the best deals, though you may need to use two or more sources before you get the type of hotel you want, at a good price.

Hotel chains in the UK

Pricing policies among the UK hotel chains (such as Holiday Inn, Thistle, the De Vere group, Hilton International and Marriott) are extremely competitive, resulting in a bewildering array of special offers, especially from the upmarket brands.

Midweek tariffs can be high, but most chains offer significantly cheaper leisure-break rates aimed at families and holidaymakers, although these often require a minimum two-night stay.

In winter 2002, *Holiday Which?* surveyed prices at UK chains by phoning the hotels directly, by contacting central reservations and by using the Internet. They found that rates could differ quite substantially. It is worth doing a bit of work to get the best deal – follow the tips in the box overleaf.

Tourist bodies

In January 2002 the British Tourist Authority (BTA) launched a campaign called UKOK to attract foreign tourists back to Britain after the foot and mouth epidemic. The promotion includes special deals on hotel rooms. Although it is aimed at overseas visitors, those living here can bag bargain accommodation too – look up **www.visitbritain.com**. At the time of writing, various room rate reductions were on offer. Deals may be available from regional tourist boards too.

Breaking the chain

- Rack rates are available in published hotel brochures or on their websites. You may be able to improve on these by phoning individual hotels.

- Armed with any alternative quotes you've obtained, ring the central reservations number and ask for the best rate they can give – some dramatic savings may be possible.

- Never be afraid to haggle for a discount. Sounding hesitant could produce a miraculous drop in rates if demand is low.

- Check exactly what terms are offered, and check your credit-card statements carefully when they arrive to ensure that the tariff and discount match what you've agreed.

- Some excellent bargains can be found on the specialist online booking systems – try the websites listed on pages 168–9

Tour operators

It's worth remembering that many tour operators, as well as agents such as Trailfinders (☎ 020-7938 3939), let you book 'accommodation only', so you don't have to go for the whole package if you are going overseas. They can some-times offer more attractive rates than you would get through contacting a hotel direct, though you may have to pay a booking fee of £10 to £30. Note also that the price is likely to be per person rather than per room, which may work out as poor value.

Single supplements

People travelling alone can end up paying pricey single supplements, often for the worst room in the hotel. Different tour operators sometimes charge different supplements for the same room, even if the hotel itself makes no charge. Although lone travellers are lumbered with this situation, there are some ways around the problem.

- Book direct to avoid paying the supplement.
- If using a tour operator, shop around for the best deal.
- Be flexible on the dates you can travel.
- Ask about weekend prices in cities with a lot of business travellers – trade will be slow then and the hotels will want to fill the rooms.
- Certain times of year (such as the period outside school holidays) are often supplement-free.
- Ask if you will get a real single or just single use of a double (there is a big difference and you may pay the same price).

Local tourist offices

The quality of tourist offices varies from country to country, though many are very good, and they often can't be beaten for local knowledge. Many of them will give you an idea of the best areas in a region, or parts of a city, to stay in, if you're unfamiliar with the area. Some offer a booking service, and will find suitable places to stay if you tell them your needs and your budget, which can be particularly useful if you're going to a country where English isn't widely spoken, and your own language skills are limited. They may also be able to offer exclusive special offers: cheap weekend breaks or deals including meals or free entry to local attractions.

Some tourist offices have very efficient websites, with comprehensives listings of places to stay – everything from small home stays to the large luxury hotels – as well as maps and information about local facilities and attractions. If you're able to get through, a phone call may yield results (most offices will have at least one member of staff with good English) but watch out for premium-rate line charges. Try Internet searches, international directory enquiries, or travel guidebooks for their phone numbers.

Travel and hotel websites

Another good place to start your search for a hotel is through some of the many travel and hotel websites. Many of these are, in effect, online hotel room brokers, which offer online booking, and their own room rates.

Useful websites
www.1800usahotels.com (USA only)
www.expedia.co.uk
www.hoteldiscounts.com
www.lastminute.com
www.laterooms.com
www.placestostay.com
www.quikbook.com (USA only)
www.travelcareonline.com
www.travelocity.co.uk
www.virgintravelstore.com

Some sites have sophisticated search features, which will locate hotels to match your budget, time of stay, location and special facilities. Many have links to the hotels' own websites, which have more information about the facilities, pictures, maps and so on. Bear in mind, though, that many of these sites have information solely (or mostly) for larger or chain hotels. If you're after smaller, cheaper or privately run establishments, you're probably better looking elsewhere.

Booking tips

Bear in mind there's no guarantee that travel and hotel websites will give you the best rates. When *Consumer Reports* (the magazine of Consumers' Union, the US consumer organisation) looked at hotel rates in the USA, it found that broker websites gave the best rates only about half the time; the rest of the time, phoning the hotel direct was the better bet. One trick *Consumer Reports* recommends if you are travelling in the US is to book several weeks ahead, and then call to check the price a few days before you're due to arrive. If it's cheaper, cancel your original booking and take the cheaper one (as long as you don't have to pay any cancellation fees).

Going direct

There's nothing to stop you contacting hotels direct. You can get names and phone numbers from recommendations in guidebooks or from local tourist offices, but the Internet means that finding hotels to contact is easier than ever, and some offer Internet-only deals.

If you are going to a relatively small town or area, you can simply search on the name of the place and 'hotel', 'pension' or 'accommodation', using one of the general Internet search engines, such as **www.ask.co.uk**, **www.altavista.com**, **www.google.com** or **www.lycos.co.uk**. This should produce some results.

In smaller hotels, pensions and bed and breakfasts, there may be a problem speaking English. But many now have email addresses, and it's often easier negotiating this way, rather than on the phone.

When contacting the hotel, always ask for the best rate. Some establishments, particularly in the USA, quote their cheap rate only if you specifically request it. It's also worth enquiring about other reductions such as off-peak or weekend rates or money off for children or senior citizens.

If you have an AA card (☎ (0870) 600 0371, **www. theaa.com**), you can use it in the USA and Canada to get discounts at hotels and B&Bs given ratings by the American Automobile Association (AAA).

General tips

Whichever booking method you use, these basic principles could save you money.

Stars in your eyes

When looking for a hotel don't get too hung up on star ratings. Doing so means you may end up paying more for somewhere to stay than you need to. Remember that rating systems differ from country to country, and stars are more about features and facilities than quality in the broadest sense. Apart from anything else, there's no point in paying to have facilities (such as room service or a swimming pool, say) that you are not going to use. It is always worth checking out the special deals at chain hotels. However, you may find a family-run two-star hotel more welcoming, comfortable and charming than a four-star hotel from one of the big chains. And you could save money at the same time.

Added extras

Paying for your room is not the end of your bills. It's worth taking a few steps to make sure that your final bill doesn't balloon.

How to lower the cost of your hotel bill

- In Europe, you shouldn't be stung by many extra taxes, but check the situation if you're travelling to the USA or Canada, for example. You may encounter a host of extras including sales, room and city taxes which can make a big difference to the final bill.
- Check whether breakfast is included in the room rate; conventions differ from country to country. (And, if it's important to you, you might want to check whether you'll be getting a simple Continental breakfast, a full-blown cooked breakfast or breakfast buffet.)
- If you'll be arriving by car, and you're staying in a city, check whether there is any free parking at the hotel. If not, find out the options and costs of nearby parking.
- Avoid making long-distance phone calls from your hotel room. Hotels have long made a killing out of such calls. Local calls are normally cheap enough (or, in some places, even free), but if you're calling long distance, use a calling card (though you may still have to pay a fee to the hotel), or use a mobile phone or public phone elsewhere.
- If the hotel has luxury facilities, such as a gym or swimming pool, check whether using them is going to cost you extra (and if so, how much).
- Try to avoid the temptations of the mini-bar. It's a convenience you'll usually pay dearly for.

CHAPTER 14

Loans

If you're looking to borrow money to finance a large purchase, you don't need to enter the murky world of the loan shark to encounter rip-off Britain – a simple stroll down the high street will suffice. When *Which?* last looked at personal loans, in December 2000, it found that a £10,000 loan from Barclays paid back over five years would cost over £1,500 more in interest charges than one arranged through Lloyds TSB Loansdirect. Clearly, it pays to shop around when you're committing yourself to a financial arrangement that often lasts for months or even years.

Borrowing – the options

Before taking out a loan you should think carefully about whether there are any alternatives. Are you in a position to borrow from your savings, for instance, and pay the money back as you would a standard loan (i.e. set up a direct debit from your current account to your savings account and effectively pay yourself back)? Or are you fortunate enough to have a cash-rich relative who would be prepared to lend you the money interest-free or at a low rate? Either option avoids the necessity of borrowing from a financial institution with the often high level of interest which that entails.

If you do need to borrow money, you have four main choices:

- getting a loan through a credit card
- getting a loan through an overdraft
- taking out a personal loan
- taking out a secured loan.

Getting a loan through a credit card

Most people don't think of the credit card as a means of taking out a loan, although that is largely what it is! The chief benefit of borrowing on a credit card is the flexibility that it allows – you can obtain instant credit on any amount up to your credit limit. And it's up to you how much to repay, although most card issuers insist that you make a minimum monthly repayment of between 2 and 5 per cent of the outstanding balance. You'll probably be charged £10 to £20 if you make a late payment or if you exceed your credit limit.

Most credit cards give you an interest-free period on purchases (up to 59 days). This means you pay no interest as long as you pay the balance in full when you get your statement. However, if you don't clear the balance then interest will be charged and this can be costly. See Chapter 8 for more details on how to look for a credit card that offers a good deal.

Credit-card interest rates are not fixed – issuers increase or decrease them from time to time. Unlike mortgage and savings rates, they don't tend to follow base rate changes.

One particular advantage of using your credit card to buy something worth between £100 and £30,000 is that you'll probably get extra protection as a result of Section 75 of the Consumer Credit Act (see Chapter 19 for more details).

Getting a loan through an overdraft

Current account overdrafts can be a good way to borrow relatively small amounts, but you need to agree an overdraft limit with your bank in advance. Some accounts let you go into the red by £50–100 with no charge to you at all. However, some charge you as soon as you go overdrawn. Overdraft interest rates vary from as little as 7 per cent to almost 20 per cent. And besides charging you interest, some accounts also charge overdraft arrangement fees, monthly fees or transaction charges when you go overdrawn, and these fees make borrowing small amounts expensive. These charges are now rare among the large high-street banks, but more common with the smaller ones (see Chapter 9 for more details).

If you go overdrawn and you have no overdraft facility, or if you exceed your overdraft limit, you will face higher charges – typically, a penalty fee and an unauthorised overdraft interest rate. You'll also be charged for unpaid cheques and direct debits.

In its most recent survey, in October 2001, *Which?* found that the following accounts offered the best-value overdraft facilities (based on the annual cost of using a £500 overdraft for two weeks a month, including any fees and interest charges): Alliance & Leicester, Cahoot, Citibank, FirstDirect.com, IF, Nationwide and Smile. Check *Which?* and the weekend newspapers for updates on the best deals.

The amount you can borrow on an overdraft is often fairly small, so you may find it easier to borrow larger amounts with a credit card or personal loan.

Taking out a personal loan

The most important thing to consider when organising a personal loan is how much you can afford to repay each month, because the consequences of not repaying a loan can be serious. Working out how much you can afford to repay will also tell you how quickly you can pay off the loan: the longer it takes to repay the loan, the higher the total cost of the loan is likely to be.

In general, you can borrow more with a personal loan than with a credit card or overdraft. Personal loan rates are fixed for the period of the loan and, as a result, so are the monthly repayments. Consequently, personal loans are good for budgeting, as you know exactly how much you have to pay each month, when the loan will be repaid and the total interest charge. Some lenders allow you to take repayment 'holidays' without penalty, although they will still charge you interest during this time.

One of the drawbacks of personal loans is that they can be inflexible, since most lenders penalise you if you want to repay the loan early. Some lenders do, however, now allow the flexibility of repaying the debt early without penalty.

Personal loan interest rates tend to be lower than other forms of unsecured lending (i.e. credit cards and overdrafts), and rates are normally lower the more you borrow. It is worth remembering that some lenders offer preferential rates to those who apply over the Internet. Look in *Which?* and the finance pages of newspapers for the Best Buys in the personal loan market.

Taking out a secured loan

If you're prepared to use your property as security for your borrowing and you have a mortgage, you may be able to borrow by increasing the size of the mortgage. Interest is then normally charged at the standard variable mortgage rate over the same term as your mortgage, although some lenders let you vary this. This is probably the cheapest form of credit you can get, but since interest rates are variable, your repayments are not fixed. And, crucially, your house is at risk if you cannot make the repayments. Some lenders let you take a further advance only for home improvements.

If you don't want, or are unable, to take out a further advance from your existing lender, you could take out a secured loan from another lender, called a second charge loan. Note that interest rates for these loans are higher than those for re-mortgaging and are around the same level as the cheapest unsecured personal loans.

If you own your home outright and so have no mortgage, a secured loan could be a viable option. You would be able to borrow a larger amount than with an unsecured loan, and pay back the loan over a longer period too, if you wished.

0 per cent finance deals

One further option, for borrowing when making purchases, is to take advantage of a '0% finance deal', which is an enticement offered by many shops. Whether or not this represents a good deal depends on whether you are confident that you can meet the repayment terms and whether the price of the goods in question is competitive. There are three types of 0 per cent finance. Always check which type is being offered.

- **Interest-free credit** You pay a deposit of around 10 to 20 per cent, followed by a series of equal monthly instalments. These repay the remainder of the purchase price over an agreed period of time, which can be anything from six months to two years. This is a good way of spreading the cost of a large purchase without paying to borrow. However, it is not an option if you cannot pay the deposit.

- **Limited interest-free credit** You pay a deposit and a series of small monthly instalments for a limited interest-free period of, for example, nine months. At the end of this period, you can pay off the outstanding balance as a lump sum or you can continue to spread the repayments over a longer period. The catch is that if you do not repay the balance at the end of the limited interest-free period, you have to pay interest on the remaining repayments. This option is worth considering only if you can repay the lump sum at the end of the interest-free period. If you can't, it is an expensive way to borrow.

- **Buy now, pay later** Rather than putting down a deposit and making monthly repayments, you pay nothing for the first few months and then pay the full purchase price at the end of the given period. No interest will be charged. However, you will be asked to sign a credit agreement when you buy the item, which usually gives you the option to extend the credit period (at extra cost) if you cannot repay the full amount (or you forget to pay the full amount). The credit company may not remind you to pay because – unsurprisingly – it would rather you paid the interest. This sort of deal is best avoided if you cannot or are likely to forget to repay the amount in full at the end of the period.

How to compare deals

Once you know what your borrowing options are, you will need to compare the cost of loans from different lenders. The first and most important thing to ascertain is that the monthly repayment is affordable. When looking at monthly repayments, look out for the extra cost of loan insurance. This can push up the cost of borrowing considerably, and can sometimes be restrictive when it comes to paying out (for example, if you become unemployed the insurer might not pay you for the first few months).

The other things you need to check are the annual percentage rate (APR) and the total cost of credit.

APR

Believe it or not, the APR is not an interest rate: it represents the total charge for credit expressed as a percentage and enables you to compare the real cost of loans of the same type. As well as the interest you pay, it also takes into account any fees and charges you have to pay for arranging the loan, any compulsory insurance you have to take out, the amount and frequency of the loan repayments, and the length of the loan.

Although the APR helps you to narrow down your choice of loans it does not tell the whole story, because different assumptions are used when calculating the APR for different types of credit. This is not a problem if you are comparing two loans of exactly the same type (e.g. one personal loan with another) with exactly the same duration and repayment schedule. However, if you want to compare the cost of a personal loan with the cost of a credit card, for example, the APR will not help. This is because the APR for a personal loan takes into account the fact that the amount you owe gradually goes down as you make your monthly repayments. With a credit card, the APR is calculated by assuming that the amount you borrow stays the same until you pay it in full and that you pay only interest throughout the duration of the loan. This difference in assumptions can have the effect of making a personal loan that charges the same rate of interest as a credit card look cheaper than using a credit card and gradually paying off the loan each month.

However, as a guide in this type of comparison: if the credit-card APR is the same as, or lower than, the APR for the personal loan, the credit card will give you the better deal provided you gradually pay off the loan.

Total cost of credit

The 'total cost of credit' (or 'total amount payable') has to be included on all advertisements and marketing material for personal loans – although not credit cards. This tells you the total amount you will have paid out by the time you have finished paying off the loan.

Useful contacts

The following are just some of the price-comparison websites that you can use to help you find the best deal for your particular circumstances.

www.ftyourmoney.com
www.moneyextra.com
www.moneyfacts.co.uk
www.moneynet.co.uk
www.moneysupermarket.com

If things go wrong

If you have difficulty in resolving a complaint that you have against a lender, you should first of all follow their own internal complaints procedure. Failing that, you can contact the Banking Ombudsman Scheme, ☎ (0845) 080 1800, **www.financial-ombudsman.org.uk**.

CHAPTER 15

Loyalty cards, affinity cards and flight schemes

Over the last decade, the big retailers' marketing departments have busied themselves devising points schemes that appear to help us make money while we're spending it – such as loyalty cards, affinity cards and free flight schemes. But are they worth participating in? Or do they simply delude us into spending more money with no worthwhile reward?

Loyalty cards

When Tesco introduced the first UK loyalty card scheme in 1995 – its Clubcard – Sainsbury's was sceptical and dubbed it 'electronic Green Shield stamps'. It soon followed suit with its own Reward card though, as did other retailers, and by 1999 there were 40 million loyalty cards in circulation. The stores took the view that by operating these costly schemes they would benefit by encouraging customers to return and by collecting useful data on the type of purchases they made. Recently, however, there are signs that the loyalty card is on the wane with Safeway and Asda dropping their schemes in favour of straightforward discounting, which they claim their customers prefer.

The concept behind the loyalty card schemes is simple. Points are awarded according to how much you spend. In their simplest form, you use these points for a discount on future purchases at the shop in which you earned them. However, there are more sophisticated variations on the format.

Some stores have special offers, where you earn extra points by buying certain products. Sometimes you can earn and redeem points at a range of shops, using the same card (though reward rates may vary for each store). Some schemes also offer a host of discount options, such as tickets to heritage attractions, or reductions on holidays or car breakdown services – even the opportunity to donate your points to charity.

While all cards work on the same principle, individual loyalty schemes work in different ways. The most popular loyalty schemes include the following.

Boots

In addition to its basic Advantage Card, Boots offers the Advantage Credit Card in conjunction with Egg, which is a loyalty and credit card in one. It offers a good interest rate and you get five Boots loyalty points for every pound you spend in Boots (which is one more than with the standard Advantage Card), and one point for purchases made elsewhere. Each point is worth 1p. Points are not available on prescriptions and some other items.

Tesco

The Tesco Clubcard offers one point for every pound spent in the store. If you collect more than 150 points during a collection period (roughly 13 weeks) you'll be sent a voucher which works out as a penny for every point. The vouchers can be spent in Tesco or on a range of travel deals and special offers.

Sainsbury's

Sainsbury's Reward Card offers two Reward points for every £1 spent in the store. As soon as a total of 500 points is reached, a voucher is issued which can be used to obtain a discount of £2.50 in Sainsbury's. Reward points can also be used for discounts on video hire, ferry travel and energy bills.

WHSmith

With the WHSmith Clubcard, customers gain one point for every 10p if they spend over £1 and every 500 points earned will save them £1. Points can be redeemed instantly on most products (excluding stamps, tokens, phonecards, cigarettes or vouchers) and at WHSmith stores.

Useful contacts

Boots ☎ (0845) 845 4545, **www.wellbeing.com**

Tesco ☎ (0800) 591688, **www.tesco.com/clubcard**

Sainsbury's ☎ (0800) 092 1000,
  www.sainsburys.co.uk/rewardcard

WHSmith ☎ (01793) 451222, **www.whsmith.co.uk**

Pros and cons of loyalty cards

Unless you're a very big spender, it can take a long time to gain anything worthwhile – the average family spends about £2,900 a year on food at supermarkets, and the reward for this could be as little as £29. And if the same family bought all their newspapers, magazines, books, stationery and CDs at WHSmith (worth £258 a year), it would take them nearly three years to earn enough points for a CD under the retailer's loyalty scheme.

On the positive side, a loyalty card will cost you nothing and if you're a constant visitor to a particular store – most likely a supermarket – it makes sense to collect points. You'll be 'rewarded' with some money off, or, if you're not in a hurry, might find that your points add up to a handy discount off a holiday or a flight.

Chances to earn plus points

Many stores now offer special promotions, awarding extra points on certain products, rather than a straightforward price cut. They may also include other special deals, such as the supermarkets offering a relatively large number of points for opening one of their bank accounts. If you have the time and opportunity to plan your shopping carefully, there are chances for gaining points – and getting worthwhile discounts – much more rapidly than you would on standard purchases.

Affinity schemes and credit-card extras

Affinity cards and credit cards that offer specific perks reward spending, with the proceeds going to you or someone else (for information on getting a good deal on your standard credit card, see Chapter 8).

Affinity credit cards

These offer the chance to make donations to a selected charity or cause as a result of your card usage. When you first take out the card, a certain amount (usually between £5 and

£10) is donated to the relevant charity. Thereafter, the charity gets a small percentage of each purchase you make – roughly 0.2 to 0.5 per cent.

There is a diverse range of affinity cards on offer – the market-leading Bank of Scotland (☎ (0800) 454235, **www.bankofscotland.co.uk/creditcards**) alone has more than 500 – and you can choose to benefit organisations as diverse as major charities, your former university or even a football club.

Although the percentage that gets donated to your chosen cause is very small, the amounts do add up over time. The Comic Relief card, which was originally launched by the People's Bank and is now operated by Citibank (☎ (0870) 010 7610, **www.littleredcard.co.uk**) has raised well over £100,000 within a period of roughly two years.

Affinity cards are certainly worth considering if you are committed to a particular cause or organisation. But bear in mind that being charitable can have its price, as affinity card interest rates can be some of the highest in the market. If you pay off your balance in full each month, that's not a concern. But if you always maintain a balance on your credit card, then you'd be better off looking at a more competitive card and setting up a regular direct debit payment to the cause of your choice.

Credit cards with perks

Looking for a credit card with attractive extras makes sense if you pay off your bill in full each month, since a competitive interest rate will probably not be as important to you as it is to those who borrow on their card. Below we list some of the perks that may be offered as part of a credit-card package.

Points schemes

With some credit cards, you earn points according to how much you spend. These can be exchanged for goods, or discounts on goods. Research among *Which?* subscribers has found that this is by far the most widely used perk among consumers. Examples of this include the card from GM (☎ (0870) 600 0234, **www.gmcard.co.uk**), which offers discounts on the price of a new Vauxhall car (one *Which?* subscriber who saved for two and a half years on this sort of scheme earned a discount of nearly £2,000). The Goldfish card (☎ (0800) 885555, **www.goldfish. co. uk**) allows you to get discounts on British Gas bills as well as at a range of high-street retailers, and Barclaycard (☎ (0870) 154 0154, **www.barclaycard.co.uk**) offers 'profile points' which you can exchange for products from its catalogue.

Points schemes are potentially useful if you actually want the goods on offer and spend enough on your card to accumulate the necessary points.

Purchase protection

Some cards provide insurance against the damage, loss or theft of goods you buy with the card. Typically, cover lasts for 90 or 100 days from the date of purchase, but the level of cover varies, depending on the card issuer. Purchase protection can be a useful perk, but it is important to check first – you may already be covered by your house contents insurance policy.

Travel accident cover

This is offered by most credit-card issuers when you pay for travel using the card. It covers you if you die or are seriously disabled while travelling, with the maximum cover limit

---

Redress for credit-card shoppers

Don't confuse purchase protection with your rights under the Consumer Credit Act. Section 75 of this Act allows you to claim from your card issuer if any goods you buy with your credit card are not delivered or are faulty. For more on shopping rights, see Chapter 19.

---

usually between £50,000 and £100,000. However, it does not cover your other travel insurance requirements, such as the loss or theft of your possessions. As a result, it's of limited value to most people who require comprehensive travel insurance when they go abroad.

Free card registration

This enables you to make just one phone call to cancel all your cards if they are lost or stolen. Free card registration is generally offered with 'Gold' cards. You also get card protection insurance to cover any fraudulent spending before you report the disappearance of your cards. The ability to cancel all your cards with one call is useful, though the insurance element is not a valuable perk as your liability for fraudulent use is limited to £50, and once you've told your card issuer that the card is missing you are not liable for further losses unless you have been grossly negligent (you have written your PIN number on the card, for example).

Replacement cards

Most credit-card issuers offer an emergency replacement card, which will be sent to you if yours is lost or stolen while you are abroad. Many issuers will also provide you with emergency cash if you lose your cards while you're abroad. These can be very useful features.

Air Miles

The Air Miles scheme offers you the chance to collect points when you make purchases which are redeemable against flights with British Airways, British Midland and Go, and against holidays with jmc, Cosmos, Airtours and First Choice. Approximately six million people take part in this massively successful incentive scheme.

You can collect Air Miles by:

- using a Nat West, Ulster Bank or Air Miles credit card. Remember, though, that you have to be a serious card user to claim free flights. For example, you have to spend £9,000 with the cards that give Air Miles in order to get a flight to Paris worth about £70

- buying petrol at Shell garages, where you can exchange Shell Pluspoints for miles (you'll need to buy 375 litres of petrol over 3 months to gain 25 miles)

- using a Sainsbury's Reward Card – 500 Reward points can be exchanged for 40 miles. On this basis a return flight to Paris would require a spend of around £3,000

- spending with more than 350 businesses such as energy suppliers, car hire companies and retailers. However, accumulating Air Miles does not necessarily mean a good deal overall on your utility bills. *Which?* found in November 1999 that energy tariffs which feature Air Miles as a perk are more expensive than the cheapest deals available. A year's energy bills could feasibly pay for a flight to Paris, but most of these would have been awarded as an incentive to sign up. See Chapter 12 for how to save money on energy bills.

If you want to redeem your Air Miles on a flight, you can either spend them on the entire flight or on a 'part miles/part cash' basis, so that you use up fewer Air Miles but pay a sum of money as well.

For more information about Air Miles, phone ☎ (0870) 557 7788 or look up **www.airmiles.co.uk**.

Air Miles come down to earth

As with any 'free' perk – and in common with other frequent flyer schemes – there are plenty of catches associated with Air Miles collection.

- You'll be required to pay the normal airport taxes as well as other fees and charges.
- Air Miles are generally redeemable only on off-peak services, and booking is bound by flight capacity so you might not be able to get a seat on the flight of your choice. It's therefore best to book some way in advance. For advice on the best way to book a cheap flight, see Chapter 1.
- Changes to bookings cannot generally be made.
- Flights are restricted to a minimum of a one-night stay and a maximum of one month.
- Air Miles are not normally transferable (though they can be bequeathed in a will).
- If you use Air Miles to pay for a flight or holiday and then have to make a claim for cancellation, you may find that your travel insurance company does not cover you. Check with your insurer that it provides cover for Air Miles.

CHAPTER 16

Mortgages

Buying your home is probably the biggest financial commitment you'll ever make, though few people find the subject of mortgages as fascinating as looking round the houses or flats they might buy with one. By doing a bit of research and choosing the right loan you could save yourself thousands of pounds. Sadly, in recent years, there's been widespread evidence of people getting poor or downright misleading advice on the best mortgage for their needs.

Don't end up with the wrong mortgage

Choosing a mortgage involves two key decisions: which deal is best for you, and how you repay the loan. There are more than 100 mortgage lenders, most of them offering a range of products with different interest rates and features, so it's no wonder potential borrowers are confused. But whether you go straight to a lender (such as a building society or bank) or get a mortgage through a broker or other 'intermediary' (such as an estate agent or independent financial adviser) you need good advice on the best type of mortgage for your circumstances. Poor advice may mean you end up with a loan which isn't as cheap or as flexible as another you could have got.

The Mortgage Code says that an adviser should make clear to you what sort of service they are offering. This may range from information about a single mortgage product to a recommendation about what would suit your particular situation. However, the Code is only voluntary and evidence shows that it hasn't solved the problem of bad advice – though some changes are now under way (see pages 195–6).

Types of mortgage

There are two basic ways of repaying a mortgage:

- A simple **repayment** mortgage, where each month you pay back some of the loan as well as interest on the amount outstanding. Provided you keep up with your monthly mortgage payments, this method guarantees that your mortgage will be paid off at the end of its term.

- An **interest-only** mortgage, where you pay just interest to the lender, but don't repay any of the loan until the end of the mortgage term. To make sure you have a sufficiently large lump sum to be able to clear your mortgage debt, you also pay into some form of long-term savings plan. In the past, the most common investment used to back a mortgage was an 'endowment' policy, although these days the majority of lenders recommend using an ISA (Individual Savings Account). Using the lump sum from a personal pension is also an option, but one which isn't suitable for many people. You should take independent financial advice before deciding on this route. Whichever type of investment you choose, the proceeds from it are meant to cover the whole of the capital sum you borrowed in the first place – however, this is not guaranteed as many endowment policy holders have found to their cost.

Which? has found that in terms of how much you pay out altogether, one way isn't significantly better value than the other (*Which?* May 2001 gives typical comparison figures).

But only a repayment mortgage can guarantee that the debt will be repaid in full.

A lender's basic mortgage product will usually be at what's called the 'standard variable rate' (SVR) which goes up and down as bank interest rates change. Beyond this, many lenders may offer cheaper rates, and there may be a variety of special deals which set out to attract customers by, for example, offering a low rate of interest in the first few years:

- **Fixed-rate mortgages** These guarantee that the rate won't change for a stated period – say from two to five years. This means you don't have to worry about increased payments in the first few years when money may be tight. On the other hand, if the lender's SVR falls below your fixed rate, you will lose out.

- **Discounted-rate mortgages** These are at rates which go up or down but for a stated period are always, say, 1 per cent lower than the SVR.

- **Capped-rate mortgages** With these, the interest rate is guaranteed not to rise above a certain level during the capped period, which is often between three and five years. If the lender's SVR falls below the capped rate, you pay the SVR. A 'capped and collared' mortgage sets a minimum as well as a maximum rate for the specified period.

- **Cashback deals** With these you get a percentage of the loan – say 5 per cent – as a cheque to spend on financing your move or whatever you choose. Smaller cashbacks are often offered as part of a fixed- or discounted- rate deal.

- **'Mix and match' deals** These let you borrow part of your mortgage at a variable rate and part at a fixed rate –

letting you hedge your bets to some extent on whether interest rates go up or down in the future.

- **Tracker mortgages** These exactly follow the bank base rate plus a specified percentage margin.

Many of these deals – especially ones which look good value at first glance – may have strings attached, which are often tucked away in the small print. For example, there may be hefty 'redemption penalties' if you repay your loan early or switch to a better deal in the early years of the mortgage. Redemption penalties can be high – it could mean repaying all the savings you have made on a special deal, for example. Alternatively, the lender may require you to take out your house insurance or payment protection insurance through them. *Which?* has called for this practice to be banned.

Flexible, current account and offset mortgages

Some lenders now offer 'flexible' mortgages which give you more freedom to repay at the speed you choose. You may be able to make small increases or decreases in monthly payments, or pay fortnightly, or take 'payment holidays' where you pay nothing for a few months, or increase the amount of the loan. But you're unlikely to be able to combine flexibility with a very cheap rate. Current account mortgages (CAMs) and offset mortgages let you link your mortgage to a current account and savings account and essentially use your savings to reduce the size of the mortgage on which you pay interest. CAMs combine everything into one account, whereas offset mortgages keep your accounts separate, making it easier to keep track of your finances.

Problems with mortgage advice

Mis-selling of endowment mortgages has gained a lot of publicity in recent years. Many people were sold policies which failed to cover the amount owed. This type of mortgage is now fairly uncommon, but other problems can still arise. *Which?* surveys have found (see *Which?* May 2001) that getting good mortgage advice is a hit-and-miss affair:

- Some mortgage intermediaries are tied to just one company's products, so can't give comprehensive or independent advice (though the Mortgage Code says they should inform you of this).
- Some advisers don't fully assess borrowers' needs and circumstances (such as whether they expect to be able to pay off part of the loan as a lump sum after a few years).
- Some don't spell out the differences between repayment and interest-only loans, or make misleading claims that repayment mortgages are poor value because you don't pay off much of the loan in the first few years.
- Some advisers fail to explain redemption penalties fully.
- Mistakes by mortgage companies have also resulted in some borrowers unwittingly paying off just the interest on their loan, because a suitable policy to repay the capital wasn't set up for them – see *Which?* July 2000.

The Mortgage Code

The Mortgage Code is a code of practice which aims to improve the standard of mortgage advice and service from lenders and intermediaries. Although it's voluntary, all consumer mortgage lenders subscribe to it and will only deal with intermediaries who also sign up. For a copy of the code, ask your lender or adviser or contact the Mortgage Code Compliance Board (☎ (01785) 218200, **www.mortgagecode.co.uk**).

Under the Code, lenders and intermediaries can offer three levels of service: information on a single mortgage, information on the different types of mortgage offered, or advice and recommendation. Advice and recommendation means the adviser assesses your specific needs and recommends a suitable mortgage. The lender or inter-mediary should tell you at the outset which level they are offering. If you're not told, ask – you will have more of a comeback if you hit problems after going for the advice service.

Unfortunately, it's not possible to recommend where you should go for the best advice, as *Which?* has found that the advice you get depends on the individual you happen to speak to rather than the company he or she works for. The good news is that in December 2001, the government announced that the Financial Services Authority (FSA) will regulate mortgage advice. At the time of going to press, the plan is that regulation of advice will start in 2004.

Where to get mortgage advice

It's best to contact a range of different sources. Building soci-eties and banks are the main lenders and all will have liter-ature and websites you can look at, and branch advisers you can talk to. Some have also set up 'direct lending' operations which work by phone or the Internet rather than through branches, and may offer preferential rates. Insurance companies may also be in the mortgage market and a property developer or builder may be able to arrange loans in the case of a new house. Then there are mortgage brokers or 'intermediaries' such as estate agents or financial advisers who make arrangements for you to borrow from someone else. Some are tied to one finance company and sell only that lender's products; some have links to a handful of lenders; and some are fully independent. If you pay the intermediary a fee you are more likely (but not guaranteed) to get impartial advice. With a repayment mortgage, you may have to pay a fee to the broker; with other types of mortgage the broker gets commission for arranging the savings plan set up to pay off the loan when it matures.

Mortgage comparison sites

Charcolonline **www.charcolonline.co.uk**

Creditweb **www.creditweb.co.uk**

Fred Finds **www.fredfinds.co.uk**

Moneyextra **www.moneyextra.com**

Moneyfacts **www.moneyfacts.co.uk**

Moneynet **www.moneynet.co.uk**

Money Supermarket **www.moneysupermarket.com**

UK Mortgages Online **www.ukmortgagesonline.com**

The Internet is potentially a good place to compare the thousands of mortgages available. Many sites offer calculators and comparison guides to help you decide which type of mortgage is best for you, as well as explaining all the jargon. But as with any advice, some sites offer a limited selection, and only a few are truly comprehensive.

Tips for a best buy mortgage

- Check out a variety of types of lender and adviser, including direct lenders which operate over the phone or Internet, as well as high-street banks and building societies.

- Before you go to see an adviser, think about what your long-term plans are – for example, are you likely to want to move to a bigger property within a few years?

- What percentage of the purchase price do you want to borrow? If you want to borrow more than 90 or 95 per cent, the lender may impose a fee (which could be several hundred pounds) for 'mortgage indemnity guarantee' insurance to protect itself should you default on the loan.

- Be prepared for the adviser to ask you about your attitude to financial risk. This will affect whether an interest-only loan is suitable for you and if so which investment would be best for you Remember that in this case, the small print may state that it's you, not the lender, who is responsible for checking that a suitable ISA or other investment is in place to cover the loan.

- Get written statements of all the payments involved. Watch out for small print which requires you to buy house insurance or mortgage payment protection insurance from the lender.

- Look for a lender which calculates interest daily or monthly rather than annually. Over a 25-year mortgage term this could save you several thousand pounds. And it also makes it easier to vary your monthly payments.

- Watch out for longer-than-average redemption penalty periods, or other penalty clauses which may be attached to cheap-rate mortgages. Some redemption penalties apply only for the duration of a special deal, others may

lock you into the lender's SVR for a number of years afterwards.
- If you think you'll want to switch lenders or pay lump sums off early on, avoid deals with redemption penalties. You can now get special deals, such as discounted- or fixed-rate mortgages, without redemption penalties. Alternatively, try for a 'mix and match' deal where most of your loan is at the discounted rate and, say, £10,000 at the standard rate. The standard part of the loan won't have a redemption penalty period, so you could pay off this amount in lump sums without a fee.

CAT standards

These are government standards (CAT is short for Charges, Access and Terms) for mortgages. These standards are a benchmark which should ensure a reasonable-value mortgage with no hidden charges or terms – for example, one condition is that interest is calculated daily (see above). But non-CAT mortgages aren't necessarily inferior. For full details of CAT standards for different types of mortgage, see the chapter on mortgages in *Which? Way to Buy, Sell and Move House.*

A better deal on an existing loan

If you've already got a mortgage, you may be able to cut the amount you pay now, or the total sum you pay over the term of your mortgage. If you're in the early years of your mortgage, check first that you won't have to pay a redemption penalty which would wipe out any useful saving. You have several options listed below.

Switch your mortgage

In many cases you could save money by switching to a different scheme with your existing lender, or to a more competitive lender (see 'Tips for a best buy mortgage').

Cut your mortgage term

Many mortgage advisers let you assume that all mortgages are for 25 years. This isn't so. By cutting the term from 25 to 20 years you'll have to pay more each month, but this may be less than you think, and if you can afford it you will end up saving thousands of pounds in interest. With inflation low at present and tax relief on mortgage payments abolished, it makes sense to pay your loan off early if you can. Most lenders won't charge for shortening the term in this way.

Repay a lump sum

If you have a sizeable amount of spare cash (over and above what you need to keep for emergencies), you may be better off using this to pay off some of your mortgage (unless you have a heavily discounted mortgage rate) than putting the money in a savings account. You'll cut the outstanding amount on which you're paying interest and, if you stick to the same monthly payments, you'll pay off your mortgage sooner.

Pay off more each month

If you don't want to commit to cutting the term of your mortgage, consider making regular or occasional monthly 'overpayments' instead. But check that your lender calculates interest by the day or the month. If your lender calculates interest annually (and some lenders still do), you won't benefit from any overpayments you make until the end of their financial year. If this is the case, put the money in a high-interest savings account and pay a lump sum once a year.

Making a complaint

If you're dissatisfied with the advice or service you have received from a lender or intermediary, you should first take it up in writing with the firm concerned. The Mortgage Code says firms must have their own internal complaints procedure. You can get a copy of the Mortgage Code from your lender or intermediary, the Mortgage Code Compliance Board, or the Council for Mortgage Lenders.

If the internal complaints procedure does not resolve your complaint, you can refer it to either the Financial Ombudsman Service or the Mortgage Code Arbitration Scheme. The firm should tell you which of these applies to them. Both schemes can examine the evidence, make a judgement and, if appropriate, recommend that the lender pay you compensation of up to £100,000.

For details about making a complaint, go to the Financial Services Authority website (see opposite).

Useful contacts

Council for Mortgage Lenders ☎ 020-7437 0075,
www.cml.org.uk

Financial Ombudsman Service ☎ (0845) 080 1800,
www.financial-ombudsman.org.uk

Financial Services Authority ☎ (0845) 606 1234,
www.fsa.gov.uk/consumer

Mortgage Code Arbitration Scheme ☎ 020-7421 7444,
www.arbitrators.org

Mortgage Code Compliance Board ☎ (01785) 218200,
www.mortgagecode.co.uk

CHAPTER 17

Perfume and aftershave

The perfume market is considerably more open now than it was in the 1990s. Then, as with the domestic utility monopolies, consumers were often faced with the choice that was no choice. If you wanted a particular perfume you were restricted to buying it from an outlet authorised by that perfume house and that authorised outlet did not discount heavily.

During the 1990s, however, a number of important victories were won by some retailers, most notably Superdrug, to be able to sell perfumes to consumers at lower prices. The perfume houses argued that their customers wanted the special ambience and service offered by trained and smartly dressed staff. They also maintained that they spent millions of pounds on research, development and marketing and wanted to protect their brand image by keeping their products exclusive.

When you examine what you actually pay for in a perfume then the cost of exclusivity and image is plain to see. As *Which?* reported in December 1998, in general a £30 bottle of fragrance costs about £3 to manufacture, £10 to market, package and distribute. It is estimated that there's room for a retailer mark-up of over 30 per cent, £9-plus in this case.

Where to shop

You can buy perfume from a variety of sources.

The high street and specialist shops

Superdrug (**www.superdrug.com**) has been at the forefront of trying to break the price control of the perfume houses. Since 1991 it has been attempting various tactics, such as importing on the 'grey market' (legitimate goods imported without the authorisation of the manufacturer) to sell at discounts of around 30 per cent. Superdrug can now source authorised stock from some firms at reasonable prices.

Your local high-street chemist can also be a good hunting ground for discounted perfume and cosmetics.

Also worth a look is the specialist chain The Perfume Shop. It has more than 70 branches around the country (☎ (01494) 539900 to find your nearest one), and it also sells through its online store (**www.theperfumeshop.com**).

Supermarkets

The major supermarkets have also taken a tilt at the perfume market from time to time. Unlike the specialists and Superdrug, they have been less consistent and tend to have limited stock. However, their discount offers can be up to 75 per cent off the original high-street price. The two supermarkets most likely to offer discounts are Asda (**www.asda.co.uk**) and Sainsburys (**www.sainsburystoyou.com**). Keep your eyes peeled on your weekly circuit round the supermarket or check in the press for advertised special deals.

Buying online

The Internet is a good place to find discount perfumes. However, you tend to have to know what you are looking for, and not every brand is discounted. Perfectly Priced Perfumes (**www.perfectlypricedperfumes.co.uk**) and

Fragrance Direct (**www.fragrancedirect.co.uk**) both have
well-designed sites that boast special offers and decent search
engines.

Take care if buying from overseas

You may come across online perfume discounters, based in
the USA, offering tempting prices on your favourite scent.
Remember that you'll have to pay delivery charges from the
USA and probably also duty, which together may wipe out
any savings.

If you know exactly what you want, and simply want to get
the best price possible, online shopping fits the bill. But
even if you're browsing or looking for something different,
don't be put off by 'buying blind'. Some of the sites have
guides or search engines which aim to find a range of
suitable perfumes, based on your answers to a series of
questions.

Watch for discounts elsewhere

The entry of discounters into the perfume market has, not
surprisingly, forced the more traditional retailers, such as the
department stores and Boots, to rethink their prices. Boots,
for example, does now sometimes discount certain
perfumes. Check the website (**www.wellbeing.com**) for
latest offers.

And remember that in the post-Christmas period
department stores are keen to clear old stocks of perfume
and you may find a bargain.

Duty free and travel abroad

On 1 July 1999 sales of duty-free goods in tax-free shops came to an end for people travelling between European Union countries. However, this has not put an end to airport shopping, and many UK airport shops still advertise big savings over high-street perfume prices. Check out other sources before assuming that duty free is the cheapest option. The perfume houses control how the duty-free stores retail their products, and the price reductions are not always as good as those found in the discount stores in the UK and online.

If you are travelling further than Europe you can sometimes find significant savings. Airports in Asia and the Middle East in particular often have a vast array of shops – and keen prices. For example, prices at Singapore's Changi airport were about a third less than UK high-street prices for a range of popular perfumes.

You can also get good deals in other countries for perfumes and toiletries. The USA and France tend to come out well for many cosmetic products. Some of this is simply greater competition in those countries, some of it product positioning.

CHAPTER 18

Rail tickets

There was a time when travelling by train was simple: you bought a ticket from British Rail, and that was that. But, as we all know, privatisation has seen an end to all that. The privatisation process, which started in 1994, was supposed to bring private-sector efficiency and competitiveness to the rail industry. Choice, better service and cheaper rail fares were all promised.

However privatisation has, in many ways, been little short of a catastrophe. The breaking up of British Rail into dozens of companies, including Railtrack and the train operation companies (such as Virgin, GNER and Connex) has, by most measures, seen performance decline. The fragmentation of the network and the way in which it is regulated is widely considered to have led to a lowering of safety standards. Reliability and quality of information have declined, while cancellations have increased leaving rail travellers confused and frustrated. True, more consumers now travel on the trains, but the sad fact is that a lot of this is because of the prolonged economic boom in the UK rather than any improvement in the railways – more economic growth triggers more train travel.

Why we pay so much for rail tickets

The unfortunate truth is that, overall, we in the UK pay over the odds to travel by train compared to consumers in Europe and the rest of the world. And the splitting up of British Rail has left a fiendishly confusing fare structure, which cannot possibly be understood without the aid of a computer.

High ticket prices

For some types of tickets, most notably 'walk-up' fares – where you pay just before you travel – prices are now enormously high. So high in fact that it is often cheaper to fly, either within the UK or indeed abroad. A few years ago who would have thought, for example, that you could fly from London to Amsterdam for less than you could catch a train from London to Ipswich? But no-frills airlines have been selling such return flights for £43, compared with £44 for a standard return on the train to Ipswich.

Variation in fares

Under the old British Rail there was a relatively simple system of discounted fares. These tended to be centred around offers for those travelling outside peak times or for those in certain demographic groups, such as students, pensioners and families. But now that the rail companies are run as private businesses, which have to maximise their turnover (and profits), they increasingly sell their tickets like airlines. This is called 'yield management' and works on the basis that seats have no value once the train has left the station. Tickets thus tend to be sold on a more complex system that tries to get the most money out of the customer for the seat that is sold. So just as airlines charge higher prices at times of high demand (Friday evening for popular business destinations, the summer school holidays for holiday destinations, for example), so too are the rail companies now selling tickets according to demand. In other words, they will charge (up to a point) what they can get away with. While this had started to happen at the end of the British Rail tenure, it was always balanced with a fair dash of public service combined with ineffective marketing.

However, the fare that you end up paying on the railways is even more complicated than the one you pay on an airline, because certain fares are 'regulated' – the rail companies are required by regulations to offer certain types of fare. This mix of market and regulation is the main reason for the fantastically confusing fare structure we now have. The statutory representation body for passengers, The Rail Passengers Council (RPC), reckons there are currently 90 different types of rail fare in the UK.

What this complexity also means is that the difference between the cheapest and most expensive fares is often greater (in percentage terms at least) than the cheapest and most expensive seats on a plane, in the same class. For example, you could pay as much as £180 for a return standard-class ticket from London to Glasgow – or as little as £24.

Cutting the cost

There are several ways around the problem. The first is simply to choose not to use the train. Travelling by coach is generally a cheaper option, if slower and less comfortable long-distance. Contact National Express (☎ (0870) 580 8080) for details of routes around the UK, or look up the deals on **www.gobycoach.com**. An increasing number of internal flights can undercut internal train journeys. However, you have to know how to work the airline ticket system as well as the rail system to take advantage of this route. For information on cheap flights, see Chapter 1.

If you do want to let the train take the strain there is a silver lining in the dark cloud of privatisation. By doing your homework, and if you're prepared to be a bit flexible, you can pick up bargain fares on long-distance trains, which were previously simply not available.

Ticket types

Of the several dozen ticket types that are available, some types are the same as those that used to be available when British Rail existed, and are offered by all the rail companies. These include Apex, SuperSaver and Cheap Day Returns. You can, of course, ask for a ticket by name if you think that is what you need, but the rail companies also have their own special fares, sometimes special offers, available only for short periods of time, so you are better off working out what you want, and getting rail staff to give you the cheapest fare (see 'Where to buy', opposite). But make sure you keep your wits about you as the information that you get from staff is not always correct.

Discounts

You can get discounts on rail tickets with a Railcard, which you can buy at most stations, and which last for a year. There are different railcards available for young people (under 25), people with disabilities, elderly people (over 60) and families (people travelling with children under 16). There is also a Network Railcard, which gives discounts if you are travelling in the south-east of England.

For more about these ticket types and Railcards it is best to look at the website of the rail companies, **www.nationalrail.co.uk**. The Rail Passengers Council also has information at **www.railpassengers.org.uk**. If you don't have access to the Internet, it will send you a leaflet (☎ 020-7713 2700).

Where to buy

One of the problems with getting the best fare is that getting good advice on the best fare can be a hit-and-miss affair. In January 1996 *Which?* investigated the quality of information being given by the National Rail Enquiry Service (NRES), the centralised train information service. Although NRES is an accurate source of information about where and when different trains run, nine out of ten times researchers were given the wrong information when they asked about the cheapest fare for a range of journeys. On average, the quoted cheapest prices were £24 more than they should have been.

Sometimes the problem was because staff simply didn't know about all the discounted ticket options, and sometimes because they didn't know that there was more than one way of getting to the destination, and that some routes were cheaper than others. Remember that the poor staff often have to contend with enormous books of fares plus special offers, leaflets and tie-ins with newspapers. Bear this in mind when you request fare types. Note also that although fare information can be obtained, you cannot buy a ticket through NRES.

NRES and the rail companies say they have invested a lot in improving this, but finding the cheapest fare still isn't easy. But where you buy from can make a difference.

From a station

In theory, you should be able to buy a ticket to and from anywhere on the national rail network from any ticket office in the country. But if your local station is not a main station, staff there are unlikely to be able to search for all routes and options to find the cheapest fare for you for a complicated journey, or for one that is in another part of the country. Your local rail company is likely to be most interested in selling its own services.

Main stations – the larger stations in big cities and the London termini – should have all the information at their fingertips (and staff should be used to dealing with complicated itineraries).

It could be worth calling NRES first to find out your options, and get a quote for a fare. But whether you do this, or simply turn up at the station, there are several things you should do to make sure that you're getting the best deal possible – see 'Tips for cheap tickets', page 214.

Over the phone

You can book tickets over the phone from any of the rail companies. Most let you do so only if you are going to be travelling on their own trains, which is fine for local journeys or if you know that the rail company is the only one that you can use for the route you want to take. But if you're doing a longer journey, where you're not sure which company to use, or you have a choice of companies, or your journey will involve a lot of changes, you need to beware.

All train companies will let you book tickets for their own trains over the phone, and six of the train companies (see 'Useful contacts', page 215) have booking services which let you plan your journey and pay for tickets anywhere in the country. They offer 'impartial' advice, which means that they should offer you the tickets and fares that suit you best, whichever rail company they are with. But, as with buying a ticket at a station, make sure you're not paying over the odds (see 'Tips for cheap tickets').

If you are booking by phone, you need to be able to pay for tickets with a credit or debit card, and tickets are normally posted out to you. If you are travelling within a few days, or if you would prefer to, you may be able to pick up tickets at the station you are travelling from, but you can do this only at certain stations.

On the Internet

The best bet for finding the cheapest fare is probably to use the Internet, if you can. A couple of websites let you plan a journey and book online: **www.thetrainline.com** (operated by Virgin) and **www.qjump.co.uk** (operated by National Express, and also available through the websites of several train companies – see 'Useful contacts', below).

Like phone bookings, the services are impartial, and you have to pay with a debit or credit card, and have the tickets posted to you (unless you are travelling from a station at which you can collect the tickets).

Of the two services, thetrainline is the most helpful. You key in details about where and when you want to travel, including any particular routes you want to take, and it comes up with a list of possible fares. The useful thing is that it gives you a complete list of possible options, so you can look at the fares available on different trains, as well as journey times and the number of changes, and work out which one suits you best. For example, it might make clear that, if you were prepared to travel half an hour earlier than you had planned, you might be able to save £20 on your ticket. Or you might get a better choice of discounted fares if you can travel back a day later than planned.

Once you've decided on the route, time and fare that suit you, you can check the conditions of the ticket (restrictions such as whether you can change or cancel the ticket) before you buy.

The Qjump service offers the same routes, and sells tickets at the same prices, but it doesn't provide the infor-

---

Useful contacts

Timetable and fare information (any journey)
National Rail Enquiry Service (NRES) ☎ (0845) 748 4950
Timetable and fare information and bookings (any journey)
Anglia Railways ☎ (0870) 040 9090
First Great Western ☎ (0845) 700 0125
GNER ☎ (0845) 722 5225
Midland Mainline ☎ (0845) 712 5678
ScotRail ☎ (0845) 755 0033
Virgin Trains ☎ (0845) 722 2333

Websites for timetable and fare information and bookings
www.thetrainline.com
www.qjump.co.uk

Websites for UK train companies

Anglia Railways	**www.angliarailways.co.uk**
Arriva Trains Northern	**www.northern-spirit.co.uk**
c2c	**www.c2c-online.co.uk**
Central Trains	**www.centraltrains.co.uk**
Chiltern Railways	**www.chilternrailways.co.uk**
Connex South Eastern	**www.connex.co.uk**
First Great Eastern	**www.ger.co.uk**
First Great Western	
	www.great-western-trains.co.uk

---

mation in the same way, so you don't get an at-a-glance guide to your options.

Tips for cheap tickets

Follow these tips to make sure you get the right ticket at the right price.

First North Western	**www.firstnorthwestern.co.uk**
Gatwick Express	**www.gatwickexpress.co.uk**
GNER	**www.gner.co.uk**
Heathrow Express	**www.heathrowexpress.co.uk**
Hull Trains	**www.hulltrains.co.uk**
Island Line	**www.island-line.co.uk**
London Underground	**www.thetube.com**
Merseyrail Electrics	**www.arriva.co.uk**
Midland Mainline	**www.midlandmainline.com**
NI Railways	**www.nirailways.co.uk**
Scotrail	**www.scotrail.co.uk**
Silverlink Train Services	**www.silverlink-trains.com**
Stansted Express	**www.stanstedexpress.co.uk**
South Central Trains	
	www.southcentraltrains.co.uk
South West Trains	**www.swtrains.co.uk**
Thameslink Rail	**www.thameslink.co.uk**
Thames Trains	**www.thamestrains.co.uk**
Virgin Trains	**www.virgintrains.co.uk**
Valley Lines	**www.valleylines.co.uk**
WAGN	**www.wagn.co.uk**
Wales and Borders Trains	
	www.walesandborderstrains.co.uk
Wessex Trains	**www.wessextrains.co.uk**

- If possible, use one of the Internet booking services to see what's on offer. You don't have to book your ticket online if you don't want to – you can simply work out what the cheapest fares are, and buy elsewhere.

- If you can't use the Internet to check fares, think about when and where you want to travel and, more importantly, how flexible you can be before trying to book your ticket. Prices can vary greatly depending on the time of day you travel, so think about how important it is that you leave (or arrive) by a certain time. If you can be flexible, always ask if there is a cheaper ticket travelling at a different time.

- If you are taking a long or complicated journey, ask if there is a cheaper route, even if it takes longer (for example, travelling from London Marylebone to Birmingham on Chiltern Railways may be cheaper than taking a Virgin train to Birmingham from London Euston).

- Make sure you are clear about restrictions on your ticket before you pay (the trains or train companies you can use, and whether you can change your ticket or get a refund if you can't travel).

- If you are taking a long journey through the south-east of England, it can be cheaper if you avoid London (though your journey may take longer).

- If you are not confident that the person you are speaking to is answering your questions, or is giving you the best advice, try another source (see useful contacts).

CHAPTER 19

Shopping rights

A bargain is no bargain at all if it breaks down, doesn't work properly, or isn't what you ordered. So before you get mesmerised by cheap prices you need to know your rights and what you should be aware of when, for example, ordering over the Internet or ordering cheap items from abroad.

When trouble strikes

If a product you've bought in the UK is faulty, you should first complain to the retailer you bought it from or, if it is under guarantee (see box below), to the manufacturer. They may fix it for free or replace it without an argument. When you contact them you must be clear about what you are asking for. Legally, you are entitled to your money back or to compensation (see 'What the law says', below). However, many retailers will offer a repair or replacement, even though they are not obliged to. If you have suffered additional loss as a result of the product being faulty (for example, if you had to throw out food which was spoiled because your freezer broke down) then you should also claim compensation for this loss.

If the retailer won't do what you want, don't be daunted or fobbed off. Sometimes just making a shop know that you are aware of your legal rights is enough to make it sort out the problem. If not, you may have to threaten – and then take – legal action.

Taking legal action normally means using the small claims track (in England and Wales), if the value of your claim is less than £5,000, or the sheriff court (in Scotland). These courts are quite informal and are organised so that you can put your own case. You can get forms and more details from your local county court (see 'courts' in your phone book), Citizens Advice Bureau or legal advice centre, or at **www. courtservice.gov.uk**. You can also start a claim online through **www.courtservice.gov.uk/mcol/index.htm**.

What the law says

The most important law covering goods and services is the Sale of Goods Act 1979 (amended and strengthened by the Sale and Supply of Goods Act 1994). This states that goods you buy must comply with the following conditions (among others).

- Goods must fit any description given (for example, on the label or packaging or in an advertisement). So a 'waterproof' jacket really must be waterproof.
- Goods must be of 'satisfactory' quality. This means they must be in good condition, safe to use, strong enough to last a reasonable length of time and have no faults.
- Goods must be 'fit for the purpose'. This includes any purpose you made clear when you bought or ordered them, as well as the usual purposes for which the goods are used. So if you told a shop that you wanted a printer that would connect to your type of computer, the printer should do this.
- Goods must match any sample you were shown. So if you order a sofa, its fabric must match the fabric you were shown when you ordered it.

In all parts of the UK except Scotland, if a purchase does not meet these conditions you are entitled to make a claim up to six years from the date of purchase. In Scotland the time limit is five years from the time the fault in the product became apparent. However, it is advisable to act as soon as possible – legally, you are only entitled to a *refund* if you reject the goods within a 'reasonable' time, and this is actually very short – often just a couple of weeks. Beyond this time you are legally entitled only to compensation (usually the cost of repair).

Remember that these rights are against the retailer, not the manufacturer. The retailer is whoever sold the product to you – this could be a shop, market stall, mail-order company or website. The retailer cannot pass the buck by telling you to contact the manufacturer about a fault. You can complain to the manufacturer if you want, especially if the product is covered by a guarantee (or if the retailer has gone out of business) – but you cannot use the Sale of Goods Act to take the manufacturer to court.

You can claim against the manufacturer if you are claiming for loss or damage caused by defective goods, rather than for the goods themselves – for example, if your TV exploded and caused a fire which damaged your carpet, and you wanted compensation to replace the carpet. In this case, you would use the Consumer Protection Act 1987 (but to claim, the loss must be over £275).

If you simply decide you don't like something, or it doesn't suit you, a shop may give you your money back or give you a credit note to use on some other item. But, legally, a retailer doesn't have to do either of these things. The law on refunds and replacements applies only if something is faulty.

New European Union (EU) consumer protection rights were due to come into force in 2002 as we went to press. This will mean that if a fault in a product appears within six months of purchase, you will be entitled to a repair or a replacement, unless the retailer can prove that the product wasn't faulty, or that it couldn't reasonably be expected to last that long. You will also have the right to some or all of your money back if:

- the product can't be repaired or replaced, or it is not practical to do so; or
- repairing or replacing the product is considered to cost too much, taking into account the type of fault it has.

This directive will be implemented in the UK by amending the Sale of Goods Act and other relevant legislation. This will mean that, in addition to the current rights (that you are entitled to reject faulty goods and, if within a 'reasonable' time, claim a refund, or, if later than this, to claim compensation) you will also be entitled to ask for the goods to be repaired or to have them replaced. Under the current rules, your right to compensation lasts for six years (or five years in Scotland). It is likely that the government will decide that your new rights will also last for six years, although under the EU directive these rights to repair and replacement must be exercised within two years.

Buying things privately

The parts of the Sale of Goods Act which say that something must be 'of satisfactory quality' and 'fit for the purpose' don't apply to private sales (i.e. sales from a person, not a business such as a shop). Here the legal principle of 'buyer beware' applies, so you should check something carefully before you buy.

Guarantees and warranties

Many products come with a guarantee or warranty from the manufacturer. This may promise, for example, a free repair or replacement if the product goes wrong within a year. There is no legal difference between a guarantee and a warranty. If the goods are still under guarantee when a fault arises, using the guarantee may be the easiest and quickest way to sort out a problem.

Any benefits given by a guarantee are in addition to your rights, under the Sale of Goods Act, against the retailer – they do not replace or undermine them. This is why you will often see the phrase 'this does not affect your statutory rights' with a guarantee or on a receipt, for example. And you will still have your Sale of Goods rights even after the guarantee has run out.

However, you do have some rights when you buy privately. Even private sellers must not 'misrepresent' items by misleading you or lying to you about something. So, for example, a person selling a second-hand car must not give you false information about its age or mileage. If you are misled by a private seller, you may be able to claim compensation from him or her – although this is easier said than done.

Buying at auction

In theory, the Sale of Goods Act applies to auctions. But in practice its main conditions may not apply if there is a notice on display at the sale or in a catalogue which excludes them. And if you buy something at an auction, your rights are against the seller, not the auction house, and the seller may be difficult to find. Also, your statutory rights can be limited at an auction, whereas they can't be when you buy from a business.

Buying second-hand

Your rights also apply to second-hand goods, although the law says you must take into account the price you have paid, and be prepared to have lower expectations of quality. For example, it wouldn't be reasonable to expect a 10-year-old, high-mileage car to perform as well as a brand new one, or to last as long.

Buying in sales

You have the same rights to a refund or compensation (and, once the EU directive is implemented, to replacement or repair) with a product bought in a sale as with a non-sale item. However, if the sale item was reduced in price because of a fault that was made obvious in the shop, or was pointed out to you (for example, a chip in a vase), you won't be able to get a refund, for example, because of that fault.

Buying by mail order or over the Internet

The law under the Sale of Goods Act applies equally to buying by mail order or over the Internet (or indeed by any other channel, e.g. by phone) as to buying in shops – as long as the retailer or website is based within the UK. The Distance Selling Regulations (see 'Buying from abroad', below) apply to sales made from any EU country, including the UK, and provide extra protection for consumers who purchase goods by mail order or over the Internet. However, if you are buying over the Internet it still pays to make some checks on the web trader before you part with your money. This is particularly important if it is a non-UK or non-EU site.

- Look for 'real world' contact details. A phone number and postal address as well as an email address on the site show that the company really does exist and is happy to be contacted. Be aware that just because a site has UK in its website address, this does not mean that it is based in the UK.
- Check that the site is secure. When you are in a secure part of a site (usually the page where you give your credit-card details) a security symbol will appear on the screen. Usually this is a key or closed padlock on the browser toolbar or the letter 's' in the Internet address after the 'http' prefix. The security information should be easy to access on the site. If you are not satisfied that the site is secure, ring the listed phone number and arrange to pay by more conventional means.
- Study the website and email address carefully. Unscrupulous sellers may make their address as similar as they can to one used by a well-known company by simply adding a couple of letters.

Buying from abroad

You need to keep your wits about you when buying from other countries. You do not have the same rights as in the UK, and it can work out more expensive than you expect.

Legal protection

A set of laws called the Consumer Protection (Distance Selling) Regulations 2000 give you legal protection when buying from any EU country by mail order, fax, over the phone, on the Internet, or through a TV shopping channel.

However, they don't cover auctions (or online auctions), or buying from countries outside the EU – which of course includes the USA. When buying from non-EU countries you have to rely on whatever local consumer protection laws apply in that particular country.

These regulations state that you must be given certain information about your order and the company you are dealing with (such as the name and address of the supplier; the price, including tax and delivery charges; and information about your right to cancel an order) before you buy. More importantly, you must also be given protection against fraudulent use of your credit-card details, and a 'cooling-off period' – which means you can cancel your order, without having to pay anything. (If the seller has sent written confirmation of, and information on, the contract, then the buyer can cancel within seven working days – from the date of delivery of the goods or receipt of this information, whichever is the later. If this written confirmation is not sent, the buyer has three months in which to cancel.)

The regulations don't cover everything you might buy. Package holidays, financial services (loans and investments, for example) and food are three of the main things that are not covered. Financial services are completely exempt. The regulation of most financial services and some financial products is the responsibility of the Financial Services Authority (FSA) – for contact details see page 202. Holidays and food are mostly exempt but some of the regulations still apply – i.e. in relation to credit cards, complaints and inertia selling (where unsolicited goods are sent to a consumer). For more on holidays, see below.

Certain types of goods are also excluded from the right to cancel the contract: these include goods that are liable to deteriorate rapidly (e.g. flowers); audio or video recordings if

the seal has been broken by the buyer; newspapers and magazines; and gaming, betting and lottery services.

Checking out the real cost

The USA in particular has proved attractive to online
shoppers, sometimes simply because there are products there
not available in the UK, but often because advertised prices
for some items can be dramatically lower. But shopping
abroad – especially in non-EU countries – requires extra
caution.

To begin with, if there is a fault with a product bought
from abroad, sorting it out could be a major headache. Some
things (electronic goods, for example) come with an international guarantee, so you may be able to get the problem
fixed here. Otherwise, enforcing your legal rights in another
country can be extremely difficult, and, in any case, not practical – even for something costing a few hundred pounds.

The second thing to consider is delivery times: if you
make a large order, you must choose between either
expensive airmail or courier delivery, or something cheaper
that could take weeks or months. If the same item is available
in the UK for a bit more money, the convenience of buying
here may well outweigh the possible savings if buying from
abroad.

Finally, you've got to be careful with prices. That bargain
price you see on a US website could well balloon by the
time the item reaches you, eating into (or even wiping out)
any savings on local prices. As already described, you will
have to pay for delivery, which can be pricey – especially if
you want the item quickly, or if it is heavy or bulky. You may
also have to pay duty and VAT. Whether you have to pay
these, and how much duty you have to pay, depends on what

you're buying and where you're buying from. You don't have to pay duty or VAT on books, so they are a particularly good option. But on other products you could have to pay up to 17 per cent duty, plus 17.5 per cent VAT. So, for example, something with an advertised price of £100 could end up costing you £137.47 – plus delivery.

Delivery problems

If you buy something by mail order (which includes over the phone or on the Internet) from an EU country, the Distance Selling Regulations (see above) say that your order should be delivered within 30 days, unless you agree to something different. But these regulations don't apply if you order something in person (for example, in a shop). So if you do this, agree a delivery date with the shop, and if possible get them to put it in writing (e.g. on the order form).

It always makes sense, however, if you are buying from any overseas country, to check that there is an indication of delivery times with your order – and an email address, and preferably a phone number, through which you can check the status of your order.

The credit connection

If you pay £100 or more for something on credit, the Consumer Credit Act 1974 gives you rights against the credit provider (for example, the credit-card company or, if you buy through a personal loan or hire purchase, the bank, building society or finance company) if there is a problem with the goods. This means that, along with the retailer, the credit-card company or credit provider is equally responsible for sorting out any faulty product or one that doesn't get delivered – so you can complain to the credit-card company/provider if the retailer won't help you. This is especially useful if the retailer has gone out of business.

Remember that the Consumer Credit Act applies to credit cards, but not to charge cards or debit cards, such as Switch or Delta. Many card companies will take responsibility for purchases from abroad made by credit card, but there is some debate as to whether the law as it stands covers purchases made abroad.

Problems with holidays

The main risk you need to insure against when buying a bargain flight or holiday is of the agent or holiday company going bust – either after you've paid, or when you're abroad. Holiday companies (even large, reputable ones) can, and do, go bust, so it's worth taking some steps to make sure you won't be left out of pocket. Some recommendations for airlines are on page 21.

There are a range of 'bonding' schemes which cover you if there are any problems with the company you've paid money to. This means that you should get your money back if the company goes bust before you go on holiday, or you will be able to get home (or continue your holiday) if the company goes bust while you're away.

Check whether any company you are thinking of buying from is a member of any of the DTI-approved schemes (see below). If you have any doubts at all about a company, contact the scheme to check whether the company really is a current member.

If you pay for your holiday by credit card, you will normally also be able to get your money back from the card company if the holiday company goes bust. Be aware that, technically, in order for you to be covered the credit-card slip should be made out to the airline or tour operator, for example, not an agent. However, some credit-card companies promise a refund even if the payment is made to the agent.

DTI-approved bonding schemes

Air Travel Organiser's Licence (ATOL) ☎ (020-7453 6430, **www.atol.org.uk**

Covers all flights, except scheduled flights bought directly from the airline or from an agent that issues your ticket on the spot.

Association of British Travel Agents (ABTA) ☎ 020-7637 2444, **www.abta.com**

Covers many travel agents and tour operators.

Association of Bonded Travel Organisers Trust (ABTOT) ☎ 020-7930 2388, **www.abtot.com**

Covers small or medium-sized companies whose packages don't include flights (mainly coach holidays).

Association of Independent Tour Operators (AITO) ☎ 020-8744 9280, **www.aito.co.uk**

Covers companies whose package holidays don't include flights.

Bonded Coach Holidays ☎ 020-7240 3131, **www.bondedcoachholidays.co.uk**

Covers coach holiday operators.

Federation of Tour Operators (FTO) ☎ (01273) 477722, **www.fto.co.uk**

Covers some of the major tour operators, including Airtours, First Choice, Thomas Cook and the Thomson groups.

Passenger Shipping Association (PSA) ☎ 020-7436 2449, **www.cruiseinformationservice.co.uk**

Covers package holidays that start and finish at a UK port.

Yacht Charter Association (YCA) ☎ 023-8040 7075, **www.yca.co.uk**

Covers yachting and boating hire companies worldwide.

Useful contacts

The Office of Fair Trading ensures that consumer legislation and regulations are properly enforced and provides information to help consumers understand their rights ☎ (0845) 722 4499 **www.oft.gov.uk**

The Department of Trade and Industry's 'Consumer Gateway' website (**www.consumer.gov.uk**) provides online access to information and advice for consumers, from government departments, consumer organisations and others.

CHAPTER 20

Telephones and mobiles

Despite years of competition in the fixed-line telephony market and a rash of offers in the mobile phone market, there is still a long way to go before we have a phone system of which we can be proud. The industry structure remains skewed by the position of British Telecom (BT) in the market. The power of BT has waned but it still has a huge 71 per cent of the domestic fixed-line market. Perhaps more significantly, because it provides the network backbone for rivals it has a central role in allowing competition to develop.

The sheer complexity of offers available in the mobile phone market is enough to give you a headache, even if the ring tones don't! At the time of writing the mobile phone companies are being challenged by their industry regulator, the Office of the Telecommunications Regulator (OFTEL) over their 'call termination' charges (i.e. the charges you pay for calls between networks) and by the European Commission for 'roaming' charges (those you pay when abroad).

In both the fixed-line and mobile telephony markets it is worth considering carefully what sort of consumer you are or are likely to become, including in your assessment how much use you will make of the Internet. You will need to do a little homework, but *Which?* and the industry regulator have done a lot of the groundwork.

The basics

In both the fixed-line and the mobile telephony sectors, there are three basic factors to take into account when choosing your telephone company:

- line rental
- the cost of calls
- the extras bundled in the service.

Don't be put off by the thought of having to change your telephone number. You're entitled to keep your old one when you switch companies – although your new company might charge you for the privilege.

For fixed-line telephones you might also have to pay a fee if a new line or cable has to be installed. Find out who your local cable company is and ask how much it will charge you for a fixed line. Three cable companies operate across much of the urban UK: Telewest ☎ (0800) 953 9000, **www.telewest.co.uk**), Eurobell – part of Telewest ☎ (01752) 300300, **www.telewest.co.uk/eurobell**) – and NTL (☎ (01256) 752000, **www.ntl.com**). You can find out if one serves your area by entering your postcode on their websites or phoning their customer services departments.

The fixed-line market

According to OFTEL – the industry regulator – 93 per cent of UK consumers have a fixed telephone line service at home. Until recently, choosing which company you used to make calls was reminiscent of Henry Ford's maxim: you could have any one you liked as long as it was BT. Now, however, the market appears to be enormous, with any number of companies making claims as to how much cheaper their calls are than the competition. In reality there is BT and there is the rest – a hodge-podge of very small operators nibbling away at the margins of BT. The depressing fact is that this explosion in competition has led to 'confusion marketing'. This tends either to snare lazy customers – who don't analyse these companies' claims or look at the small print – or serves as a deterrent for many people who could make potentially large savings by switching phone companies.

Although you can now choose the company from which you rent your telephone line and the company you pay for your calls, around 8 out of 10 UK phone users still pay BT for both line rental and calls. The best savings, however, are often to be made by using a combination of companies. Your options will depend on your circumstances, and on the companies that operate in your area.

Line rental

Roughly 50 per cent of UK phone users live in areas with access to cable services and can therefore choose to rent their phone line from a cable company rather than from BT. Alternatively, they can switch to a calls-and-access provider such as Servista (☎ (0870) 241 2732, **www.servista.com**). The OFTEL website **www.phonebills.org.uk** has information on switching. The smaller companies rent their lines from BT, and bill customers directly for line rental and calls.

The cost of calls

You don't have to use the same company for both line rental and making calls.

Indirect companies, such as OneTel (**www.onetel.co.uk**) and Superline (**www.superline.co.uk**) offer calls – but no line rental. You can use them for some or all of your calls and continue to rent a line from your main phone company. To access an indirect company you'll either need to enter a code, dial a freephone number, or use a special autodialler (a small box that re-routes your calls). The largest savings to be gained from using indirect companies are usually on international and national calls.

If you're a BT customer, you can take advantage of various discount schemes and packages, usually in return for a higher rental fee. Ring your phone provider and get a breakdown of the offers available to you.

The extras

Make sure that you check out any 'extras' that are thrown into the service, particularly when you are thinking about signing up for a cable service. For example, there may be a bundled telephone and cable TV package. This may enable you to access more TV channels for the same price that you may pay just for a line rental. There may also be an Internet-related offer, such as an unmetered access part of the bill.

Choosing the best deal

Once you know what the basic elements of your phone bill will be, including your estimated use of the Internet, you can start shopping around for the best package. It is worth bearing the following tips in mind.

Let someone else do the legwork for you

OFTEL coordinates a price-comparison service site (see **www.phonebills.org.uk**) that includes details of the main direct operators' prices. You can enter your phone bill details to work out how your company compares with another. This is a great place to start to find out if it is worth switching. The site will also provide details of how to contact the companies concerned.

Remember that price isn't everything

What's the point of getting discounts on calls if the company you switch to gets its billing wrong, fails to connect you or has an erratic service? The Telecommunications Industry Forum produces six-monthly leaflets giving details of phone companies' performance. These leaflets tell you whether orders were completed on time; the number of faults reported and how quickly they were repaired; customer satisfaction with complaints handling; and customers' views on billing accuracy. The leaflets are available from public libraries or by looking at **www.cpi.org.uk**.

Check the small print

Be sure to check the small print of any telephone deals that look enticing. Some companies round up your call to the nearest minute, rather than charging per second. For instance, if a call lasts six minutes and two seconds, you'll be billed for seven minutes. Also, beware of minimum charges or connection fees if you tend to make a lot of short calls. While a company might offer 1p-a-minute calls, it may also have a minimum call charge of around 5p a minute – meaning that a 1p call is impossible.

Another problem might be that some of the cheaper deals from indirect operators offer worse voice quality than you're used to. (Unfortunately there is no way to check this in advance.) Also, some indirect services can only be accessed with an autodialler (see above) which you have to pay for.

Be wary of comparison claims – for instance, 'save 50% compared with BT standard rates'. These claims are often based on comparisons with peak-time rates and do not take BT's many discounts into account.

Check conditions on payment methods

Some companies might offer different rates if you pay in advance or into a special account. If you set up such an account you might be required to pay by direct debit. With certain prepay deals, companies automatically top up your account – either by credit card or direct debit – by an amount agreed with you in advance. You need to be sure that you are comfortable with this and keep an eye on it to make sure that it suits you in the longer term.

Using the Internet as a phone service

Although it's not an alternative to a fixed-line service, you can make big savings on international phone calls by using your PC and a headset to speak, via the Internet. The downsides are that voice quality is very poor, and the services can be difficult to use, with time delays a major problem. That said, if you make regular long-distance calls and are confident using a computer, you might like to check out companies such as Net2Phone (**www.net2phone.com**) or Iscom (**www.iscom.net**). A *Which?* survey in January 2000 found the former to be cheaper for calls to Australia and France while the latter was cheaper for calls to the United States.

Mobile phones

Barely a decade ago, mobile telephones were regarded as an executive gadget, even if the gadget was the size and weight of a housebrick! Nowadays, the majority of us (about 40 million) – even schoolchildren – own one and no bus or train journey is complete without the chirruping of a novelty ring-tone. Unfortunately, the mobile phone market is beset by complex and confusing tariff structures, and internal cross-subsidies. This makes it difficult to compare offers.

The basics

There are three choices to make when it comes to choosing how you want to pay for a mobile phone:

- prepay (also known as pay-as-you-go)
- contract (which includes a line rental)
- no line rental.

Decide how often you're likely to use the phone before choosing which sort of tariff is best for you.

Prepay

Prepay tariffs are usually the simplest and tend to be the cheapest for low users. Their launch changed the profile of mobile phone use, opening up the market to teenagers and those without good credit histories. They appeal to people who do not want to be tied into regular payments – in fact, more than two-thirds of mobile users prefer this type of arrangement. You pay in advance for the phone and pay for calls in advance by buying vouchers (usually between £5 and £75) or by credit or debit card. Vouchers are on sale in a large number of retailers. There's no separate connection fee, credit check, contract or monthly bill. However, the per-minute call charges tend to be more expensive than other tariffs. Some tariffs also have a daily charge which eats into your credit, even if you don't make calls.

When deciding whether prepay is right for you, you have to weigh up the advantages – no credit check or direct debit payments – against the fact that the call charges are higher than with a contract arrangement. Generally speaking, if your call charges are £20 or more each month and you're likely to use the phone for more than three minutes each day, you'll probably save money by arranging a contract. Of course, if you do not have a bank account this option is not available.

If keeping up with the latest model of phone is important to you, then it's probably best to avoid prepay. The latest models are often 'free' as part of a contract but expensive with prepay.

Two types of prepay tariff are currently available.

- **Traditional charging structures** These set call charges depend on the time of day you make your call. Calls at peak time – usually between 7am and 7pm – cost more than those made in the evening and at weekends.
- **Stepped tariffs** These don't take into account the time of day. You pay one rate for the first few minutes of calls each day and then a lower rate for calls made after that.

Before you choose a package, look at the individual charges very carefully. Does it offer, for instance, free calls to voicemail or are you likely to spend a lot of credit picking up your messages? Note that all packages have very high charges for calling a mobile on a different network. If you're going to make regular calls to a particular mobile, it makes sense to choose a package from the same network. If you have a group of friends that regularly talk to each other it is worth trying to get everyone on to the same network.

Quality and performance across the networks is generally good but reception can vary between different areas. Mobile phone shops should have maps showing reception quality (or look on the individual networks' websites) and you can ask the advice of friends or family living in the area.

What sort of prepay user are you?

In a report published in December 2001, *Which?* categorised users into three categories:

- 'careful users' use their phone in the most cost-efficient way, so they stick to off-peak hours
- 'spontaneous users' use their phone whenever they want to – whatever the time of the day and whatever the cost
- 'emergency users' don't use their phone very often. When they do, it's to arrange meetings or let family or friends know where they are. However, this could be at any time of day.

This report analysed prepay packages and found that the best bet for 'careful users' was BT Cellnet's Pay & Go Original. 'Spontaneous users' were advised to look at Carphone Warehouse's Fresh Freedom tariff (up to 128 minutes a month), Virgin (128 to 213 minutes a month) and One 2 One's Standard tariff (213 minutes-plus). The best buy for 'emergency' users was Carphone Warehouse's Fresh Freedom tariff (up to 50 minutes of calls a month). The Fresh tariff charges per minute; the other networks charge per second. If you make lots of short calls (less than a minute), Fresh will not be the cheapest option.

Contract

Paying for a mobile phone by monthly contract should be straightforward. Once you've been credit-checked, you pay your monthly line rental and call charges by direct debit, and can swap between different tariffs without penalty.

All four networks – BT Cellnet (☎ (0800) 085 4103, **www.btcellnet.net**), One 2 One (☎ (0808) 121 3000, **www.one2one.co.uk**) Orange (☎ (0500) 802080, **www.orange.co.uk**) and Vodafone (☎ 07836 191191, **www.vodafone.co.uk**) – offer similar tariffs. However, they make different charges for certain services such as voicemail retrieval and itemised billing.

As an alternative to the networks, consider choosing an indirect service provider. Companies such as Telecom Plus, Dial-a-phone or British Gas buy airtime from the networks and charge their own tariffs. They may offer incentives such as free electrical items or reduced prices for other services. Check the newspapers to see how these offers get updated.

All contract tariffs include line rental for a fixed monthly fee which usually covers a certain number of free minutes each month. How many (and when they can be used) is proportionate to the cost of the line rental. A low monthly outlay of £13 might give you 300 minutes to use at the weekend or 20 minutes to use whenever you want, whereas a £25 line rental might give you between 150 and 200 minutes of calls to use any time. Take note, however, that most free minutes *exclude* calls to mobiles on other networks.

Call costs vary according to the time of day and the type of phone you're calling. Unfortunately, the definition of 'peak' and 'off-peak' varies between networks – so make sure you know when your peak and off peak times start and end – or you may make an expensive mistake as peak calls are generally more expensive. Landlines are usually the cheapest phones to call, followed by mobiles on the same network and then mobiles on different networks.

What type of contract user are you?

To take advantage of the plans available on contract phones you need to work out what sort of phone user you are. In a report in January 2002 *Which?* looked at contract tariffs and categorised users into five groups:

- 'careful users' (the same as for prepay users – see above)
- 'spontaneous users' (the same as for prepay users – see above)
- 'flexible users' who don't want to run up large bills and therefore make the majority of their calls during off-peak hours, but make the occasional peak time call if they need to.
- 'heavy texters' are spontaneous users who also send on average about six text messages a day.
- 'dependent users' make most of their calls during the day, including some international ones, and also access voicemail often.

For 'careful users', *Which?* recommended Dial-a-phone's Vodafone 300 or 600.

For 'spontaneous users', *Which?* recommended Telecom Plus's Mobile Plus (0-160 minutes), One 2 One's Anytime 200 (250-450 minutes) and One 2 One's Anytime 400 (450-500 minutes). If they use their phone between 160 and 320 minutes each month, then Vodafone 200 (plus option as above) is the cheapest.

For 'flexible users', the recommendations varied depending how long they spend on the phone each month: Dial-a-phone's Vodafone 300 (0-140 minutes), Telecom

Plus's Mobile Plus (0–160 minutes), Orange's Talk 60 (80–160 minutes), Vodafone 200 (plus option to call other networks with inclusive minutes) (140–450 minutes), One 2 One's Anytime 200 (360–450 minutes), and One 2 One's Anytime 400 (450–500 minutes).

For 'heavy texters', the recommendations were Dial-a-phone's Vodafone 300 (0–30 minutes), Telecom Plus's Mobile Plus (30–130 minutes), Orange's Talk 60 (70–130 minutes), Vodafone 200 plus option as before (130–350 minutes), One 2 One's Anytime 200 (350–470 minutes) and One 2 One's Anytime 400 (470–500 minutes).

For 'dependent users', the recommendation was Telecom Plus's Mobile Plus tariff (although if they use their phone for between 200 and 300 minutes each month, Vodafone 200 – plus option, as before – is cheaper).

As with prepay mobile phone users all of these recommendations are now dated and may well have been superseded. However, as a first step ask your mobile phone provider if it still provides the tariff recommended and, if not, what has replaced it. *Which?* will regularly update the recommendations – so keep your eyes peeled for new reports.

No line rental

The no-line-rental tariff is a tariff that lies somewhere between prepay and contract, and is used by companies such as Virgin and the Carphone Warehouse's Fresh. Users pay by direct debit, there's no line rental charge and no commitment to any contract. They receive an itemised bill every month and pay for only the calls they've made. The advantage over prepay is that users don't have to pay in advance to top up credit. However, the downside is that handsets are fairly expensive and users may still need to pass a credit check.

Useful contacts

British Gas ☎ (0845) 600 6311,
  www.britishgas.co.uk

Carphone Warehouse ☎ (0808) 100 9250,
  www.carphonewarehouse.com

Dial-a-phone ☎ (0800) 092 8244,
  www.dialaphone.co.uk

OFTEL ☎ 020-7634 8700,
  www.oftel.gov.uk

Telecom Plus ☎ 020-8955 5555,
  www.telecomplus.co.uk

Virgin Mobile ☎ (0845) 600 0070,
  www.virginmobile.com

CHAPTER 21

Toys

The problems with the toy market are many and varied but knowing what these problems are can provide opportunities to save money. This will depend crucially on the room for manoeuvre that you have with children who may have a very, very specific toy in mind. And as any parent knows, the toy market is fickle – driven by those most fickle of consumers: children.

For those toys that are 'must haves' the advice must be to get started early and shop around. Sales often outstrip production, and unless orders are placed early then disappointment is guaranteed. Try using price-comparison engines (such as **www.onlinepriceguide.co.uk**, **www.shopsmart. co.uk** and **www.kelkoo.co.uk**) to get the best price. (For more on price-comparison sites, see *The Which? Guide to Shopping on the Internet*.)

General tips

Last year's fads

The great thing about fads is that they make production planning almost impossible and they also tend to trigger copycat production. This can often lead to production overruns and overstocks. For example, the popularity of mechanical pets during 1999 and 2000 led to a glut of stock in the run-up to Christmas 2001. The response from manufacturers was twofold – go upmarket and innovate, and sell off excess stock to discounters. This move upmarket produced more high-tech and more expensive toys for 2001, while the old stock was widely available at discount stores (see below) at the same time. So, if your child liked mechanical dogs, but was not bothered by brand, then you could save money.

Take advantage of trends

Do you remember the Beanie craze of the last few years? As with all crazes this triggered a rash of imitators and look-alikes. So now, if your child is obsessed by dogs you can now buy almost any breed of dog in soft toy form. The rash of companies making Beanie lookalikes in the wake of the success of TY also led to a glut of products on the market which has generally depressed prices. In the toy market it is always worth keeping an eye on trends. Of course this can be very bad news – for example, the number of unwanted terrapins and turtles that ended up in boating lakes following the decline of the Mutant Ninja Turtle craze, or the number of people who bought dalmatians in the wake of the Disney films and did not realise that they require a lot of care and exercise. However, the film of *101 Dalmatians* has spurred the production of dog-related toys, and the popularity of Thomas the Tank Engine and the Harry Potter books and film have resulted in a resurgence in the toy-train market.

Merchandise tie-ins

The merchandise associated with specific films and TV programmes is a huge money spinner. This, of course, depends entirely on the success and popularity of the film or programme. For example, the merchandise surrounding

Harry Potter and the Philosopher's Stone has been hugely successful, while films such as *Chicken Run*, *A Bug's Life* or *Atlantis* have not been so popular. However, it is worth noting how much merchandise is released at the same time as the cinema release. Sometimes this does not sell as well as hoped and large stocks can be left around for the release of the video some time later. The most spectacular recent example of this was the over-production of *Star Wars I: the Phantom Menace* merchandise. *A Bug's Life* and *Shrek* also failed to generate the merchandise sales that were expected.

It should be remembered that younger children will often take more notice of the video release of a film than the cinema one. A canny parent will realise that some merchandise from the first release of a film can have a long shelf life that effectively lowers the demand and price of the second release merchandise. For example, merchandise from *101 Dalmatians* was still available when *102 Dalmatians* was released. So if your child yearned for a Dalmatian-related toy, you could save money by getting the earlier film's tie-in products. Discount shops source stock from earlier films in a series to sell at the same time as the new film. They also tend to get good stocks of poor-selling film merchandise. This explains the abundance of unsold *Phantom Menace* merchandise.

Note origins of TV programmes and films

It is always worth checking *where* a particular film or TV programme was made as this can give you an indication of where you might find merchandise. For example, as Babar and Asterix both originated in France, you will find a lot more merchandise for sale in France and French-speaking countries (including clothing and soft toys) than you will in the UK.

Blues Clues is another example of how you can make national differences count. *Blues Clues* is a live action/ animation mixture aimed at children of five years and under. The programme is made by Nickleodeon in both the USA and UK. Because of the penetration of the cable TV business in the USA the programme became very popular with American children around 1999. As a result, a lot of products were released for Christmas 1999. In the UK, however, because penetration of the UK TV market was relatively low for satellite and cable (the only place to see Nickleodeon and Nick Jr) there was not a sufficient market for the release of merchandise. However, in 2001 penetration of satellite and cable increased and *Blues Clues* aired on terrestrial TV in the UK. Thus by the end of 2001 there was a significant market for merchandise – but still smaller than the USA. Some UK retailers took advantage of this and imported overstocks of US merchandise and sold it at a discount.

Cultural peculiarities

While the country of origin of the toys is certainly worth checking out (see above) there are also other factors that merit investigation. For example, in France the cartoon is viewed much more as a work of art than it is in the UK. For this reason you will find in France more merchandise asso- ciated with classic cartoon figures (such as Droopy) and emphasis on the output of some of the great cartoonists such as Tex Avery. In Italy, on the other hand, the tie-in between merchandise and current film releases is less widespread and hyped. 'Classic' films and series are revered, so you will find more toys associated with older Disney movies and series such as *Tom and Jerry* than you do in the UK. Similarly in Las Vegas you will find Betty Boop merchandise at the MGM

Grand – because of ownership links. No particular reason for this exists other than cultural attitudes – but it is worth considering if you have a child who may be a Pinocchio or Tom and Jerry fan.

Where to shop

As we discussed in the section on discount clothing TK Maxx (☎ (01923 473000, **www.tkmaxx.com**) is a useful place to find toy bargains. Because of its US links TK Maxx often sources overstocks from the USA. Toy departments in TK Maxx stores vary in size and stock levels, but there tend to be good stocks of soft toys and some toys for babies.

Discount specialist toy stores can be found in a number of outlet malls and villages (for locations see Chapter 6). The most common stores in outlet villages are the Toy Factory (**www.thetoyfactory.co.uk**) and Toy World (**www.toyworld.co.uk**).

The bulk of high-street retailers price according to stock levels and fashion, so are not particularly dedicated to sourcing bargains. This is not to say that you cannot find bargains in such places.

The online toy market is also a rather small one. The collapse of etoys.com in late 2000 caused ructions in the online toy market. General retailers such as Amazon (**www.amazon.co.uk**) have a very limited stock of toys – mostly the top-40 approach to toy retailing. In contrast ToysRUs (**www.toysrus.co.uk**) has a vast stock and a bargain bin that is regularly replenished. The only problem with the latter site is that, because of its heavy reliance on graphics and its popularity, it can be slow and gets very busy at peak times. The Toy Shop (**www.thetoyshop.com**) is not, strictly speaking, a dedicated online retailer as it has a number of 'real-world' stores. The site (and shops) boasts a mixture of non-discount and bargain goods – with the site focussed on the latter. You can search by brand, price, age group and gender, which is a boon. The selection of over-stocks is wide and the reductions are significant. The Toy Centre is another useful site for end-of-stock and overstock items (**www.toycentre.com**).

Appendix:
Campaigning and
consumer action

Consumers' Association (CA), the publisher of *Which?*, isn't just about testing fridges or assessing credit-card offers. We also campaign on everything from food safety and car pricing to genetic testing and financial services regulation. You can check out **www.which.net/campaigns** to see what we are up to, and what you can do to help. We campaign in four main areas: food, health, personal finance, and retail and competition issues.

Food campaign

Consumers' Association is campaigning for all consumers to have access to food that is safe, nutritious, of good quality and affordable – and to be able to make healthy lifestyle and informed food choices.

Food labelling and licensing

We have been campaigning for better food labelling for several years, but too many manufacturers and retailers are still marketing products with misleading labels. We would like to see all catering and retailing premises reach minimum hygiene standards and be inspected before opening to cut down on the estimated 4.5 million cases of food poisoning.

Food prices

'Scrap the CAP!' The Common Agricultural Policy inflates our food prices and our taxes, and supports a small minority of big farmers. We want to see the CAP abolished and replaced with new food, rural and environmental strategies.

GM foods

Consumers are concerned over both short- and long-term safety as well as the ethical implications of genetic modification and these issues have to be addressed.

Health campaign

Debate about reform of the health service is high on the political agenda. Demands on the NHS are intense and growing as traditional public deference to health professionals is declining. At the same time, the UK pharmaceutical industry is pushing for less regulation and a greater role in health policy, and genetic technology opens up ethical debates.

Access to primary care and private health care

Roughly 90 per cent of public/NHS interaction is at the local level and many proposed NHS reforms are focused here. We have carried out a great deal of research at this level – looking at, for example, GPs, pharmacists, NHS Direct and Walk-in Centres. We have also focused attention on private dentistry by launching a 'super-complaint' to the OFT.

We have campaigned for the introduction of the Care Standards Act and the National Care Standards Commission. However, there remain gaps in the Care Standards Act, partic-

ularly in private dentistry, complementary therapy, psycho-
therapy and counselling, and the treatment of eating disorders.

New technologies

Rapid advances in technology are high on the health
agenda, with genetics technology a particularly pressing
concern. The use of genetic information by insurance firms,
and the creation of a 'genetic underclass' is an alarming
prospect.

Regulation of health professionals and redress

We are campaigning for an integrated system for dealing
with complaints about health care provided both on the
NHS and privately which meets patients' individual needs.

Drugs and treatments

Consumers' Association is campaigning against EU
proposals to relax advertising legislation for pharmaceutical
products and is calling for objective, accurate, accessible and
comprehensive patient information about medicines.

Personal finance campaign

We are campaigning for a sustainable, affordable and flexible
system that provides consumers with access to quality
financial services.

Financial advice

The financial services market is a complex and often unfath-
omable one for consumers. *Which?* research has identified
numerous poor sales practices, probably driven more by

commission rates than by consumer requirements. The sale of inappropriate financial products can hit consumers hard.

Pensions and investments

We are campaigning for a comprehensive and simplified system for saving in retirement and a flexible and safe system for providing pension income. We will also be seeking to influence policy on with-profits funds to protect existing and future policyholders' interests.

Insurance and protection

Consumers' Association is campaigning to ensure that we get high-quality, affordable insurance and protection products and services with sound advice.

Banking products and services

Retail banking competition is at the forefront of political debate. Building societies play a crucial role as a competitive bulwark against the big banks. Shoddy advice or poor practices in mortgages can be hugely detrimental.

Retail and competition campaign

Consumers' Association has spent over 40 years campaigning for retail markets that are effective, competitive and responsive to consumer needs. The challenge is no longer simply to right the wrongs in the UK, but to face the European and even global dimension of policy formation.

Digital television

Consumers' Association will be campaigning for a digital switch-over policy that enables consumers to make informed choices about going digital and ensures that early digital television equipment is fit for the future.

Car prices

UK consumers have been taken for a ride by car manufacturers for too long. CA has campaigned to lower prices in the UK and, more importantly, to change the way in which European rules that govern the sector are written and enforced. The European Commission (EC) seems to have listened.

Cutting gas prices

If you want to see how to switch gas suppliers and find out who will offer you lower prices, visit **www.switchwith-which.co.uk**.

Cheaper brands

Consumers' Association is campaigning to change EC Trade Mark rules to allow more parallel trade to give consumers cheaper branded goods.

The international dimension

Consumer issues and problems don't stop at the Channel. Consumers' Association is a member of both the European consumers' body (BEUC – Bureau Européen des Unions de Consommateurs, ☎ 00 32 2 743 15 90, **www.beuc.org**) and the international consumer body Consumers International (☎ 020-7226 6663, **www.consumersinter-national.org**). Whenever there is a European or international dimension to our campaigns we work with sister organisations to set things right.

WHICH? BOOKS

The following titles were available as this book went to press.

General reference (legal, financial, practical, etc.)

Be Your Own Financial Adviser	432pp	£9.99
420 Legal Problems Solved	352pp	£9.99
150 Letters that Get Results	336pp	£9.99
What to Do When Someone Dies	176pp	£9.99
The Which? Computer Troubleshooter	192pp	£12.99
The Which? Guide to an Active Retirement	530pp	£12.99
The Which? Guide to Changing Careers	352pp	£10.99
The Which? Guide to Choosing a Career	336pp	£9.99
The Which? Guide to Choosing a School	336pp	£10.99
The Which? Guide to Computers	352pp	£10.99
The Which? Guide to Computers for Small Businesses	352pp	£10.99
The Which? Guide to Divorce	368pp	£10.99
The Which? Guide to Doing Your Own Conveyancing	208pp	£9.99
The Which? Guide to Domestic Help	208pp	£9.99
The Which? Guide to Employment	336pp	£11.99
The Which? Guide to Gambling	288pp	£9.99
The Which? Guide to Getting Married	256pp	£10.99
The Which? Guide to Giving and Inheriting	256pp	£9.99
The Which? Guide to Going Digital	272pp	£10.99
The Which? Guide to Home Safety and Security	198pp	£9.99
The Which? Guide to Insurance	320pp	£10.99
The Which? Guide to the Internet	320pp	£10.99
The Which? Guide to Money	448pp	£9.99
The Which? Guide to Money on the Internet	256pp	£9.99
The Which? Guide to Pensions	336pp	£9.99
The Which? Guide to Renting and Letting	352pp	£11.99

The Which? Guide to Shares	288pp	£9.99
The Which? Guide to Shopping on the Internet	272pp	£10.99
The Which? Guide to Starting Your Own Business	288pp	£10.99
The Which? Guide to Working from Home	256pp	£9.99
Which? Way to Buy, Own and Sell a Flat	288pp	£10.99
Which? Way to Buy, Sell and Move House	320pp	£10.99
Which? Way to Clean It	256pp	£9.99
Which? Way to Drive Your Small Business	240pp	£10.99
Which? Way to Manage Your Time – and Your Life	208pp	£9.99
Which? Way to Save and Invest	464pp	£14.99
Which? Way to Save Tax	320pp	£14.99
Wills and Probate	224pp	£10.99
Make Your Own Will	28pp	£10.99

Action Pack (A5 wallet with forms and 28-page book inside)

Health

Understanding HRT and the Menopause	256pp	£9.99
The Which? Guide to Children's Health	288pp	£9.99
The Which? Guide to Complementary Medicine	270pp	£9.99
The Which? Guide to Managing Asthma	256pp	£9.99
The Which? Guide to Managing Back Trouble	160pp	£9.99
The Which? Guide to Managing Stress	252pp	£9.99
The Which? Guide to Men's Health	336pp	£9.99
The Which? Guide to Personal Health	320pp	£10.99
The Which? Guide to Women's Health	448pp	£9.99
Which? Medicine	544pp	£12.99

Gardening

The Gardening Which? Guide to Growing Your Own Vegetables (hardback)	224pp	£18.99
(paperback)	224pp	£12.99

Available from bookshops, and by post from:
Which?, Dept TAZM, Castlemead,
Gascoyne Way, Hertford X, SG14 1LH
or phone FREE on (0800) 252100
quoting Dept TAZM and your credit card details